An OPU

AESTHETICS

After lecturing in philosophy at Jesus and Pembroke Colleges, Oxford for two years, Anne Sheppard was a Lecturer in Classics at the University of Durham from 1978 until 1987. She then tutored in philosophy for the Open University and in 1989 joined the Classics Department at Royal Holloway, University of London, where she is now a Senior Lecturer.

OPUS General Editors

Walter Bodmer
Christopher Butler
Robert Evans
John Skorupski

OPUS books provide concise, original, and authoritative introductions to a wide range of subjects in the humanities and sciences. They are written by experts for the general reader as well as for students.

Aesthetics

*An introduction to the
philosophy of art*

ANNE SHEPPARD

Oxford New York
OXFORD UNIVERSITY PRESS

Oxford University Press, Walton Street, Oxford OX2 6DP

Oxford New York
Athens Auckland Bangkok Bombay
Calcutta Cape Town Dar es Salaam Delhi
Florence Hong Kong Istanbul Karachi
Kuala Lumpur Madras Madrid Melbourne
Mexico City Nairobi Paris Singapore
Taipei Tokyo Toronto

and associated companies in
Berlin Ibadan

Oxford is a trade mark of Oxford University Press

First published 1987 as an Oxford University Press paperback and
simultaneously in a hardback edition

British Library Cataloguing in Publication Data
Data available

Library of Congress Cataloging in Publication Data
Sheppard, Anne D. R.
Aesthetics: an introduction to the philosophy of art.
(An OPUS book)
Bibliography: p. Includes index.
1. Aesthetics   I. Title   II. Series: OPUS
BH39.S5127 1987   700'.1   87–11206

ISBN 0-19-289164-2 (pbk)

10

Printed in Great Britain by
Biddles Ltd.,
Guildford & King's Lynn

Preface

This book is an introduction to aesthetics. Although the second half concentrates on literature I hope that the book will be helpful not only to readers who share my particular interest in aesthetics and literature but to anyone seeking a way into philosophical problems about the arts.

I am grateful to the University of Durham for a sabbatical term in 1981 which helped me to get the book started and for a second sabbatical term in 1985 which put me on the way towards finishing it. I should also like to thank a number of individuals. My husband Anthony, and my parents David and Sylvia Raphael, have all read drafts of chapters and contributed many helpful criticisms and suggestions as well as giving me constant support and encouragement. Bella Wheater read a draft of Chapter 3 and made thought-provoking comments. An earlier version of Chapter 8 was read to the Philosophy Department Staff–Student Seminar at Durham University in 1982; I benefited from the subsequent discussion and particularly from the remarks of Raman Selden. Ainslee Rutledge and Farahnaz Shakoori kindly typed the final draft of the book.

August 1986

Contents

1

Why bother about art?

Here are some of the things that people do in their spare time: they read novels, they read poetry, they go to the theatre, they listen to music, they go to art exhibitions, they make trips to look at buildings or to view scenery. These are all aesthetic activities. People engage in them from choice and for their own sake. Reading a novel will not help me earn my living (unless I am a professional reviewer or teacher of literature). Going to an art exhibition will not cure me of any physical ailment. A visit to a beauty spot will not make my house any warmer. Why then do people seek out aesthetic experiences? One obvious answer would be that people do these things because they enjoy them. It gives us pleasure to read books or go to the theatre, to listen to music or look at paintings, to gaze at fine buildings or contemplate the beauties of nature. This answer tells us something, but not very much. Why seek this particular kind of pleasure? What is it about reading novels or listening to music or going to look at beautiful scenery which makes these particular activities worthwhile? There are many ways of getting pleasure: having a drink in the pub or going for a brisk walk may be pleasurable too. Why bother about art or about natural beauty? Why spend time, money, and effort on these particular sources of pleasure? Is there something special about aesthetic experiences which makes them pleasurable in some special way? Is there any further point to them, apart from the pleasure they afford us?

When we read a novel, listen to music, go to an art exhibition, or look at scenery we do not simply respond with feelings of pleasure or enjoyment. Often we want to analyse and discuss our experience. We draw attention to particular features of the novel, the music, the pictures, or the scenery. We make judgements such as 'Jane Austen shows us Emma's faults but she makes her likeable all the same' or 'The formal structure of Bach's music is particularly clear and well-marked' or 'Monet is very successful at capturing the effects of light on water and grass' or 'The combination of mountains and water makes the scenery in the West Highlands of Scotland especially fine.' What is the point of such comments? Could we justify them if we were challenged? How would such justification proceed?

We also make comparative judgements, alleging that some works or scenes are superior to others. We say that Jane Austen is a finer writer than Barbara Cartland, that Bach's music is better than what is played on popular radio, that a painting by Monet is superior to a picture postcard, that the West Highlands of Scotland are more beautiful than Blackpool. When we make judgements like this we cannot simply be talking about the quantity of pleasure we obtain. Reading Barbara Cartland or listening to popular radio gives plenty of pleasure. Is it just snobbery to declare that Jane Austen and Bach are superior? How could we defend our claims about these artists? How could we justify the statement that the West Highlands of Scotland are more beautiful than Blackpool?

All the questions I have been raising lead into philosophical problems. Broadly, there are two different ways of attempting to answer them. One is to claim that all works of art have something in common, some defining characteristic which makes them especially valuable; the beauties of nature would somehow share in this too. There is something which Jane Austen and Bach and Monet and the West Highlands have all got and which explains our interest in them. Whatever it is, Barbara Cartland and popular radio and the picture postcard and Blackpool have either a lot less of it, or none at all. Historically, different aesthetic theories have proposed different accounts of what it is that all works of art share which gives them their value. Such theories have often covered only works of art but sometimes they have been extended to include natural beauty. Three main types of theory have been proposed: the distinguishing feature of art has been held to be either imitation or expression or form. I discuss these three types of theory in Chapters 2, 3, and 4. It has also been claimed that what all aesthetic objects share is neither imitation nor expression nor form but just the quality of beauty. I consider this view in Chapter 5 together with the relevance of all four types of theory to natural beauty.

A second way of tackling the philosophical questions of aesthetics is to examine not the works of art and natural objects which we admire but the interest we take in such objects. Perhaps there is nothing special about aesthetic objects but there is a special kind of aesthetic interest, an interest which we turn principally upon works of art and natural objects but which we could direct to anything we pleased. This approach discusses the nature of aesthetic appreciation. Is there a special aesthetic attitude? Are aesthetic judgements judgements of a particular kind? These questions are considered in the second part of Chapter 5 and lead to the more specific issues discussed in Chapters 6 to 9.

This book offers a general introduction to aesthetics but I have chosen to focus on aesthetics in relation to literature. The second half of the book concentrates on literature although some consideration is given to the other arts also. Chapters 6 and 7 are concerned with critical judgements: what kind of judgement are we making when we criticize a work of art? Can critical interpretations and evaluations be justified? I pay particular attention to the relationship between interpretation and evaluation and to the question whether there is one correct interpretation of a work of art. Chapter 8 turns to the issue of meaning and truth in literature: in what sense do works of literature have meaning or convey truth? Finally, Chapter 9 considers the relationship between art and morals and in particular whether art has moral effects on its audience.

The boundaries between different branches of philosophy are not clear-cut. We shall find that some problems in aesthetics are connected with problems in other areas of philosophy, notably the philosophy of mind and moral philosophy. At the same time philosophical aesthetics risks becoming fruitless and arid if it is cut off from the realities of aesthetic experience and from the criticism of individual works of art. Discussion of examples therefore plays an important part in this book.

Rather than simply expounding the views which have been held on particular topics, I use discussion of such views to examine the problems and to develop suggestions of my own. I hope the reader will be encouraged both to challenge the arguments I put forward and to pursue further the theories I discuss. The suggestions for further reading at the end of the book are intended to help in that challenge and in that pursuit. I have tried to provide something like an aerial view of the territory of aesthetics in relation to literature. I hope that the prospect opened up is sufficiently inviting to make my readers keen to explore the country in more detail for themselves.

2

Imitation

Many works of art appear to imitate or represent things in the real world. Constable's painting, *The Hay Wain*, is a picture of a particular English landscape and art historians may identify the place where it was painted or the type of haywain portrayed and discuss how accurately Constable represents the scene (see Plate 1). Without being as specific as this we may, when we look at the painting, say immediately, 'That must be somewhere in England' or we may feel that Constable has successfully imitated or represented the subtle quality of light and colour found in the English countryside by contrast with, say, the landscape of the Mediterranean. As we shall see later, in English talk of representation often sounds more natural in aesthetic contexts than talk of imitation. The equestrian statue of the emperor Marcus Aurelius which used to stand on the Capitol in Rome represents that emperor. We may recognize it as Marcus Aurelius in particular by the beard, or by what we take to be a brooding look suitable to the emperor who was an adherent of Stoic philosophy. Literature offers similar examples: Anthony Trollope's novel, *Barchester Towers*, is treated as a realistic representation of life in an English cathedral city in the nineteenth century. The ecclesiastical historian may praise its accuracy in portraying the Church politics of the period. Without such specialized knowledge, we may well say that we know somebody just like Mrs Proudie or Archdeacon Grantly, that we recognize the type of person portrayed. We often react in the same way to drama. If we are especially knowledgeable about the phonetics and phoneticians of the early years of this century we may recognize some features of Henry Sweet in the Higgins of Bernard Shaw's *Pygmalion* but we do not need such knowledge to feel, when we see the play, that we have all met people like Higgins.

The fact that we react in this way to works of art forms part of the interest and appeal these works have for us. We like recognizing an area as 'Constable country' or identifying the sculptor's model, we find it interesting to relate *Barchester Towers* to the state of the Church of England in the nineteenth century and we enjoy the awareness that we know somebody just like a character in a play. It often seems that an artist is trying to provoke such a reaction of recognition in us and so make us interested in the work. Considerations like these have led a number of thinkers to the view that art is essentially imitative or representational, that in imitation lies the characteristic common to all works of art which defines them and gives them their value.

The view that art is imitation has a long history, for it is one of the earliest theoretical views to be held about art. Plato presents a celebrated and influential version of it in the tenth book of the *Republic*. Although Plato's main concern there is literature, he uses an illustration drawn from painting. He relates the illustration to his theory that there exist ideal Forms of many qualities, Forms of which the instances in the world of sense-experience are only copies. Thus the Form of Justice, for Plato, is the ideal which is imitated but never perfectly reproduced by particular just acts or just people. Plato speaks of particulars imitating Forms so as at the same time to convey two related but contrasting points: the particular is like the Form, for example in being just, but it is not the same as the Form; just as a copy of something is never quite as good as its model because it does not reproduce it exactly, so a particular never quite attains the ideal standard of the Form, a particular just act or just person is never perfectly just. Normally when Plato gives examples of Forms he offers Forms of qualities such as Justice or Beauty but in *Republic* X he rather unusually introduces a Form of a thing. The thing in question is a bed and he describes three levels of making and imitating. First there is the perfect Form of a Bed, made by God, then there is the bed made by the carpenter, the one which we can touch, measure, and sleep on, and finally there is the copy of a bed produced by the painter. The carpenter's bed is not only inferior to the Form of a Bed; it is even, according to Plato, less real than the Form. Correspondingly the painted bed is still more inferior, still less real. In a telling passage he says it would be easy to make everything in the world, to make it, that is, in the way the artist does: 'The quickest way is to carry a mirror with you everywhere; you will then quickly make the sun and things in the heavens, the earth as quickly, yourself and other living creatures, manufactured articles and all that was mentioned just now.'[1] The artist holds the mirror up to nature and so produces a deceptive illusion of reality, an imitation of an imitation, a very inferior product. Plato claims that literature too is imitative in exactly the same way.

This Platonic view not only offers an account of what sort of thing a work of art is but also places a value on art in general. Art by its nature is inferior, doubly removed from the true reality of the Platonic Forms, and it does not tell the truth. We might take an image in a mirror for the real thing and thus be cruelly deceived. However, it is possible to hold that art is imitation without thereby devaluing art. Later thinkers modified the theory of *Republic* X in ways more favourable to art. Even if one retains a Platonist belief in the theory of Forms, it is possible to give art a higher value than Plato did. The artist may be regarded as imitating not objects in the world of sense-experience but the ideal Form itself. The painted bed is then a copy not of the carpenter's bed but of the Form of the Bed and so will be at least equal in reality and value to the carpenter's bed. Such copying can come about because the artist perceives the ideal Form with his mind's eye. This suggestion in turn can lead to a weaker, less specifically Platonist theory that in imitating a bed the artist imitates not any actual bed made by a carpenter but some general idea of a bed which he has in his mind. In this weaker version it need not be implied that the idea of a bed in the artist's mind derives from a pre-existing Platonic Form of a Bed which has superior reality.[2]

Both the weaker and the stronger forms of this modified imitation theory have exerted significant influence on the practice of the arts. Many Renaissance artists thought of themselves as reproducing ideals in the visual form of paint or marble. Raphael, for example, in a letter to Castiglione written in 1516, said, 'In order to paint a beautiful woman I should have to see many beautiful women, and this under the condition that you were to help me with making a choice; but since there are so few beautiful women and so few sound judges, I make use of a certain idea that comes into my head.' Michelangelo in one of his poems describes how beauty 'carries the eye up to those heights which I am preparing here to paint and sculpt' and goes on to stress the folly of attributing to the senses 'the beauty which stirs and carries up to heaven every sound intellect'.[3] Such views became commonplace in the seventeenth and eighteenth centuries and were briskly mocked by Byron:

> I've seen much finer women, ripe and real,
> Than all the nonsense of their stone ideal.[4]

The theory that art is imitation is easy to understand and takes as central a feature of works of art with which we are all familiar. Hence its attraction and its wide-ranging influence. However, if we subject the theory to critical examination we shall see that it suffers from a number of weaknesses. There are two major difficulties. First of all, the theory not only claims that imitation is what all works of art have in common but also makes this the criterion of their value. Plato in *Republic* X relegates virtually all art to an inferior role just because of its imitative nature. The modified theory according to which art imitates the Platonic Form directly, or imitates an idea in the artist's mind, wishes instead to exalt the value of art and to regard as most precious that art which most successfully imitates the ideal. On any version of the imitation theory, the more successful the imitation, the better the art. Plato, at least, makes it sound as though the most successful art is the art of *trompe-l'œil* in which we are deceived into taking the illusion for the reality. Yet one might well object that even if all works of art are in fact imitative, we do not assess their success as works of art by their success in imitation. In general we do not value works of art just because they are imitative. Whether Constable's *The Hay Wain* looks like a real early nineteenth-century haywain, in a real setting, or like some ideal of an English country scene, we do not think we see a real haywain, a real river, and real trees before us on the wall of the National Gallery, confined by a canvas, and we may admire the painting for the skill of the composition, for the way the haywain on one side of the picture balances the cottage on the other, or for the soft colours, rather than as an imitation. Similarly, we may appreciate the skill with which a novel's plot is constructed, or the novelist's use of language, even if we do not find the characters 'true to life'. Imitation does not fully explain why we value works of art.

Secondly, it may be doubted whether it is even true that all works of art are imitative. All my examples so far have been drawn from types of art which can easily be thought of as imitative: landscape painting and portrait sculpture, realistic literature and drama. But not all painting and sculpture and not all literature and drama are like this. What of abstract painting? What of lyric poetry? I have said nothing so far of music. Very little music is imitative in the same sense as landscape painting, portrait sculpture, or realistic literature. Cases like the striking of anvils imitated in Wagner's *Das Rheingold* are musical 'freaks'. We would not normally say that one of Bach's Brandenburg concertos or a Mozart piano concerto or a Haydn string quartet was imitating anything.

These two difficulties require separate examination. To confront the first point, that imitation does not fully explain why we value works of art, we need to consider more closely what is meant by 'imitation' and what role imitation plays in the creation and appreciation of works of art. We have already seen that for Plato in *Republic* X imitation is slavish copying, just like holding up a mirror, and that it appears to aim at making us take the imitation for the reality. Yet this simple understanding of imitation hardly gives a correct account of the relationship between the work of art and the world which it appears to resemble. The Greek term used by Plato, *mimesis*, is sometimes translated as 'representation' rather than 'imitation'. In English the word 'imitation' implies that the copy is not the real thing. It may also imply that the copy is inferior in value. Alongside usages like 'The child is imitating someone driving a car', which implies that the child is not really driving the car, we find usages like 'This is an imitation Chippendale chair', which implies not only that the chair is not really Chippendale but also that it is of less value than real Chippendale. 'Representation', on the other hand, is more non-committal about the value of the representation and is more likely to suggest the context of art. 'The child is representing someone driving a car' still implies that the child is not really driving but suggests either some kind of dramatic context, such as a game of charades, or even the context of a picture. (The sentence might be taken as referring to a picture in which a child appears, not to a real child at all.) 'This is a representation of a Chippendale chair' has similar implications; one thinks very readily of a picture in this case. Whatever the best translation of *mimesis*, discussions in modern English of the relationship between the work of art and the world which it appears to resemble tend to be couched in terms of 'representation', thus getting away from the evaluative implications of the English word 'imitation' and making the aesthetic context clear.

Talk of imitation implies that the relationship between work of art and world is that of copy and model. Talk of representation leaves that relationship vague; fewer assumptions are made about it, but this only brings out more clearly that it requires elucidation. A change of word, from 'imitation' to 'representation', does not dissolve the problem even if it makes it look a little different. Whether we say that we are concerned with the nature of imitation, the nature of representation, or the relationship between the work of art and the world, the nub of the problem lies in the question of resemblance, of likeness. I spoke earlier, with deliberate caution, of 'the relationship between the work of art and the world which it appears to resemble'. The question is how far that relationship is really a matter of resemblance or, to put it another way, what is the role of resemblance here?

The different theories that have been put forward concerning the nature of representation in art differ principally in the role they give to resemblance. At one extreme stands the view that representation in art aims at illusion, at producing something which so much resembles its original that the spectator, reader, or audience take it to be indeed the original. We are back with the mirror of *Republic* X and the art of *trompe-l'œil*. At the other extreme stands the view that representation is entirely a matter of convention. In Western European art there is a convention that figures with golden circles round their heads represent saints equipped with haloes. Saints may be further distinguished by their individual attributes. So an eagle, for example, indicates St John and a lion St Mark. Anyone ignorant of these conventions would misinterpret many medieval and Renaissance pictures. It is possible to argue that seeing marks on canvas as a human figure at all likewise depends on conventions. The only difference is that the conventions which lead us to see the marks on canvas as a human figure are so deeply familiar that we do not realize their conventional nature. We suppose that there is resemblance where in reality there is only an arbitrarily assigned correspondence.

While the view that representation aims at illusion favours the analogy of the mirror, the view that representation is conventional tends to adopt an analogy between art and language or, more generally, between art and a system of signs. The symbols in a mathematical sign-system only have meaning by convention; so too on this view do the words in a language and the different elements in a work of art. The view that artistic representation is a matter of convention has been developed along these lines by Nelson Goodman in his book, *Languages of Art*.[5] Goodman there presents a complicated theory of how all systems of symbolic signs function and tries to show that artistic representation is a particular case of such a system.

Both these extreme views of the nature of representation are open to objection. Both of them in different ways fail to explain what is peculiar to artistic representation. I have already objected that the view of representation as illusion makes it sound as though the artist's aim is deception, as though the most successful art is the art of *trompe-l'œil*. The very fact that we can distinguish between the art of *trompe-l'œil* and other kinds of art indicates that no simple version of the illusion view can be correct. Moreover, our appreciation of a painting, for example, depends on seeing it both as a representation of something and as a set of shapes and colours; we never entirely forget that it is paint on canvas that we are looking at. When we contemplate Constable's *The Hay Wain* aesthetically we are both realizing that it portrays a particular English scene and at the same time admiring the balance of the composition and the soft colours. Indeed, it can be hard to separate our recognition that the colours are those of a typical English country landscape from our pleasure in their softness and subtlety.

The view that representation is a matter of illusion becomes even less plausible when we turn away from the visual arts. We all smile if we are told about someone who rushes on to the stage at a performance of Shakespeare's *Othello* to stop Othello killing Desdemona, for such a person has been taken in by the dramatic illusion in a way that was never intended. We may think that Shakespeare's play successfully represents the behaviour of a jealous man; what is more we may, while the play is going on, feel sorry for Othello, or angry with him, or both; we may take such feelings away from the theatre with us. Yet we do not for a moment suppose that the woman who acted Desdemona is really dead at the end: after all, she will be on stage to be killed again tomorrow. When we appreciate the play we relate events in it to events in the real world but we do not take the world of the stage to be indeed the real world. On the contrary, we know all the time that it is not. The same applies to other forms of literature: however much Dickens's original readers wept for the death of Little Nell in *The Old Curiosity Shop* they knew quite well that there was no Little Nell in the real world and if there had been, their tears would have been much less enjoyable.

The view that artistic representation is a matter of convention similarly fails to account for the peculiarities of our response to artistic representation as distinct from any other kind. It is true that the conventional symbols of mathematics and the words of a language may be the objects of aesthetic appreciation. We may consider the elegance of an equation or the pleasing sound of a felicitous phrase. Nevertheless, our main interest in mathematics and in language lies in what we can do with these sign-systems, in the use that we can make of them. By contrast we do not use the symbols of art for anything; we just contemplate them.

To say that artistic representation is a matter of convention not only risks assimilating the conventions of art to other kinds of convention; it also fails to distinguish within the sphere of art between the representational and the non-representational. We would not say that a landscape painting in which all the trees were red and the sea was bright yellow represented the colours of trees and sea even if we were given a chart which explained that this artist was painting according to a special set of colour conventions.

In the paintings of Marc Chagall we find familiar objects such as cows, violins, lovers, and bouquets of flowers but these familiar objects are associated together in distinctive and sometimes unfamiliar ways. The lovers are regularly accompanied by the bouquets of flowers and the cows by the violins; sometimes a cow actually plays a violin. These regular associations come to form a set of conventions personal to Chagall. It is precisely his use of such conventions which makes Chagall *not* a representational artist.

Just as abstract and surrealist painting have their own conventions so do imagist poetry and the novel of fantasy. As we have seen, most music is not imitative or representational, but convention plays an important part in music. To take only a few examples, there are conventions about the instruments used, about types of scale, and about the succession of quick and slow movements. Conventions may pervade a whole artistic tradition, in the way that the convention of representing saints with haloes pervades Western art, or they may be peculiar to an individual and part of his or her personal style, as Chagall's cows and violins are. Artists often react against the conventions of earlier generations. So in the twentieth century many composers have rejected the diatonic scale and have used instead the twelve-note scale which has come to provide a new set of musical conventions. Writers such as James Joyce and Virginia Woolf rejected the realistic novel of the nineteenth century and developed a new style of writing fiction. As a result the 'stream of consciousness' technique has taken its place among the conventions available to writers of novels. We shall see later that an understanding of conventions plays an important part in our understanding of art,[6] but talk of convention does not explain what is distinctive about representational art. What then distinguishes a painting with red trees and bright yellow sea from one with green trees and blue-grey sea? We seem forced to fall back on saying that in the second case the colours resemble or even copy the colours of real life and to be on our way back towards the opposite view that representation is a matter of illusionistic copying.

The truth is that understanding a work of representational art involves both a recognition of resemblance and an appreciation of convention. We know that it is only dramatic convention that Othello has killed Desdemona, yet we also see that his behaviour resembles that of a jealous husband in real life. We know that the painted haywain will never move on across the painted river, yet we admire it as a likeness of a haywain, not just as an abstract configuration of shapes and colours. Recently attempts have been made to elucidate what goes on in such understanding of representational art by means of the notion of 'seeing as'. Wittgenstein in his *Philosophical Investigations* made some remarks about 'seeing as' which have been very influential.[7] He illustrated the notion by means of various figures, including the celebrated figure of the duck-rabbit.

This figure may be seen as either a duck or a rabbit. Wittgenstein claimed that such 'seeing as' was a distinct kind of perception, different from regular 'seeing'. The application of this notion to representation in art requires considerable care. If we say simply that Constable's *The Hay Wain* may be seen as an English country scene, we have made no advance on the view of representation as illusion. If, on the other hand, we say that the configuration of shapes and colours may be seen as a representation of an English country scene, we have not really explained anything. What, we may still ask, is it to see A as a representation of B? We seem simply to have reformulated the question, 'What is it for A to *be* a representation of B?'. Yet the reformulation does bring about a significant shift of attention. It forces us to consider not the nature of the work of art but the nature of our response to it.

Suppose then that we try to give an account of what it is to see A as a representation of B. There are a number of different features of our response to representations which will have to be included in such an account. First, we do perceive some kind of resemblance between A and B although we do not mistake A for B, remaining aware of the respects in which A differs from B. We are assisted in this perception by conventions governing artistic representation: it does not worry us that the picture called *The Hay Wain* is two-dimensional and flat and has a frame round it, for we know that all this is part of being a picture. While these conventional restraints do not worry us, we do remain aware of them at some level, for when we see the shapes and colours called *The Hay Wain* as a representation of an English country scene we can at the same time see it as a configuration of shapes and colours.[8] It has been argued that this feature of our perception of representations—the fact that we remain aware of the medium of representation even while we see what it is that is represented—is better captured by the phrase 'seeing in' than 'seeing as'. We do not so much 'see A as a representation of B' as 'see B in A'; so we do not see the shapes and colours as a representation of a country scene but see a country scene in the shapes and colours.[9]

'Seeing in', however, is not peculiar to the perception of works of art any more than 'seeing as' is. We can see shapes in the clouds and pictures in the fire but we would not want to say that when we do so we are looking at artistic representations. What distinguishes the work of art here is that it has been deliberately made to be perceived as a representation. When we see an English country scene in the shapes and colours on canvas called *The Hay Wain* we are recognizing an intention on the part of the artist that we should see the shapes and colours in this way. There is more involved than recognizing the conventions that make a canvas a picture. What we are recognizing is the deliberate exploitation of those conventions. If we discovered that *The Hay Wain* had been produced accidentally by monkeys throwing paint at a canvas, our attitude towards it would change. We would then see a country scene in it much as we see pictures in the fire, assuming that such seeing is merely a projection from our own imagination which bears no necessary correspondence to a purposeful arrangement made by another.

When we respond to A as a representation of B, we are not simply deciphering a code or recognizing a resemblance. Our imagination links A and B together, guided by whatever cues the artist has included in the work. We value representational art which gives scope to this capacity of the imagination. The art of *trompe-l'œil* is not valued highly precisely because it is so easy to take the picture for the reality. There is little room here to exercise the imagination and no opportunity for the mental balancing act involved in seeing a picture both as a representation of something else and as a configuration of shapes and colours. On the other hand, a painting which claims to be representational but in which we cannot see what the title bids us see, however hard we try, fails to be successful. New styles of pictorial representation, such as Cubism, are dismissed at first because the spectators find it so hard to see what they are asked to see in them. However, once we become accustomed to making the necessary imaginative leap we may regard as especially valuable art which has given our imaginations new and exciting scope.

Just as the imagination plays an important role in shaping our perceptions of visual art, so too it has a part to play in our understanding of literature and drama. When we feel sorry for Othello, or angry with him, or when we share Eliza Doolittle's exasperation with Higgins in *Pygmalion*, we are entering imaginatively into the situation represented in the play. If we weep for Little Nell it is because we can imagine how those around her felt when she died. If we shudder at Mrs Proudie it is because we can imagine how the long-established citizens of Barchester shuddered. It is only when such an imaginative projection is possible that we speak of successful literary or dramatic representation. Suppose that, like many modern readers, we do *not* weep for Little Nell but find her death overdrawn and sentimental. If that is the case we are likely to say that Dickens's description of her death is unrealistic, that it is not a successful piece of literary representation.

The role of imagination in our response to art and the way in which it is guided by the artist's intentions will be further discussed in subsequent chapters, but we are now in a position to return to the first objection raised earlier against the theory that art is imitation. This objection was that imitation, or representation, does not fully explain why we value works of art. The objection is correct as far as it goes but we can now see that representation does, nevertheless, play some role in our valuing of representational art. It is not simple copying that we care for but the balance that is struck between copying and convention. Works which achieve that balance are valued because of the imaginative effort they demand from us.

We have still to consider the second of the two objections, that it is not true that all works of art are imitative or representational. When considering the view that artistic representation is purely a matter of convention we saw that such a view fails to distinguish representational art from art of other kinds but these other kinds of art have largely been ignored in the rest of our discussion. It is this second objection which is ultimately fatal to the theory that art is imitation.

If we take the theory that art is imitation to mean that all art is representational and that we respond to all art by 'seeing in' or other comparable forms of imaginative projection, then the theory is simply false. We may, for example, see tables and chairs in the shapes of an abstract painting but unless we either have some evidence that the artist meant us to see them, or our seeing is based on established conventions of representation, or both, this is like seeing pictures in the fire, imaginative projection without anything in the world to correspond to our projection. I have said that most music is not imitative or representational. Clearly this does not stop us using our imaginations and hearing what we please *in* a piece of music but this is not enough to show that the piece is representational. For that we would have to be able to show either that the composer intended us to hear these things in the music, or that what we claim to hear conforms to conventions of musical representation, or both.

I have been assuming so far that what is represented in art is always something in the world accessible to sense-perception: landscape, the behaviour of a jealous husband, the death of a young girl. Those who wish to defend the theory that all art is imitation or representation are forced sooner or later to widen the range of possible objects of representation. Driven to concede that there is nothing in the sensible world which an abstract painting, a lyric poem, or a piece of music demonstrably represents they may well fall back on the claim that what is represented is an emotion or a state of mind and maintain that an abstract painting in bright red represents anger or that a piece of music in a minor key represents grief. Such a use of the language of representation does not readily fit the account developed in this chapter—how could we see anger in a painting or hear grief in music?

When we see an English country scene in a landscape painting we are imagining we see such a scene, while remaining aware that we are not in fact seeing it; when we respond to the drama of Othello we are reacting in imagination to the behaviour of a jealous husband, while remaining aware that we are not in fact confronted with such behaviour. If we claim to see anger in a painting we are, it might be said, similarly imagining what it is like to feel anger. Normally when we feel anger there is a situation which gives rise to the anger and the anger is directed at some particular person or some particular thing. I may be angry with a friend or with myself; I may be angry because the train is late or because my suitcase will not shut; I may even be angry because the weather is bad, or angry with the general state of things. There will always normally be some answer to the question, 'What are you so angry about?' The anger we might claim to see in a red abstract painting, however, is just anger, not anger at anything. This is a strange kind of anger for it lacks one of the characteristics essential to anger in real life. So there are two oddities about 'seeing anger in an abstract painting', first that anger cannot be seen in the way that the English countryside can be seen and secondly that the anger lacks an object and a context.

Similarly, grief in real life has an object and normally there will be some answer to the question, 'What are you grieving for?' If we claim to hear grief in music, however, it must be grief without an object and without a context. And although we may know what a grieving person sounds like, the emotion of grief itself is not something which can be heard as soldiers marching or the striking of anvils can be heard.

To argue that emotions or states of mind can be represented is to extend the notion of representation too far. Such extension weakens it so that it becomes once again vague and ill-defined. The same applies if the language of imitation is used. It sounds even odder to say that an abstract painting imitates anger or a piece of music imitates grief than to say anger or grief are represented. We speak much more naturally of an abstract painting expressing anger or a piece of music expressing grief. What is meant by this talk of 'expression' will form the subject of the next chapter. For the moment it should be recognized that although much art is representational, not all of it is and it is an exaggeration to argue that art is to be understood simply in terms of representation or imitation. We have seen that representation requires some degree of resemblance between the work of art and something in the world accessible to sense-experience and that the best way towards understanding it lies in the study of how we respond to representational art. Such response involves both recognition of the resemblance and recognition of the conventions governing the art form; more specifically it involves recognition of the deliberate exploitation of such conventions by the artist. Representation does play a part in our valuing of representational art but since not all art is representational it cannot be representation which explains the value of all art. Even in the case of representational art, we value works which demand some imaginative effort more highly than straightforward copies. It remains unexplained how we respond to non-representational art and why we value it. To answer these questions we must consider art from other points of view, as we shall proceed to do in the next three chapters.

3

Expression

We saw at the end of the last chapter that an attempt to defend the theory that *all* art is imitation or representation would lead to claims that emotions or states of mind, not just things accessible to sense-perception, could be represented. We saw too that there are difficulties about extending the notion of representation in this way and I remarked that we speak much more naturally of an abstract painting expressing anger or a piece of music expressing grief. If we reflect on our reactions to art we shall find that many of them depend on two related assumptions: first, that one of the things artists do is express their emotions, and second, that expression is one of the sources of aesthetic value. It is these assumptions which lie behind praise of lyric poetry, for example, as spontaneous, or condemnation of it as insincere. Although many modern literary critics regard the assumptions as illegitimate they are still very common and quite deep-rooted. Our initial reaction to the short love poems of Catullus, for instance, is to assume that the poet is expressing his feelings for Lesbia and we may be quite taken aback when a critic shows us how the impression of spontaneous emotion is achieved by skilful manipulation of imagery, language, and metre.

With music too we readily fall into assuming that the composer is expressing emotions which he genuinely feels. Some of the effect of Peter Shaffer's play, *Amadeus*, comes from the shock which both the audience and the characters in the play feel at the contrast between the civilized and beautiful music of Mozart and the vulgarity and ugliness of the composer's personality as depicted by Shaffer. Often the amateur finds a purely technical criticism of a piece of music in terms of harmonies, themes, and variations hard to follow, and is glad to fall back on talk of 'the joyful second movement' or 'the longing expressed in the finale'.

The assumption that art is expressive is perhaps less pervasive in the visual arts. Here our first reaction is often to see things in representational terms and we may seek to find representations of familiar things in the shapes of an abstract painting. Although we do speak of paintings as 'sad' or 'cheerful' or 'serene', when we refer to emotions in describing visual art we are frequently more concerned with the emotions evoked in spectators. So we may speak of 'a disturbing painting', 'a depressing building', or 'a statue which suggests calm and repose'. Literature and music also evoke emotions in their audiences and often the way an audience responds to a work is taken as indicating which emotion the author or composer was expressing. In considering expression we shall be concerned not only with the relationship between a work of art and its creator but also with the relationship between a work and its audience.

Although the idea that art involves the expression of emotion may be traced back to ancient thought, it was the eighteenth- and nineteenth-century Romantics who made it all-important.[1] It is to their stress on the emotions of the artist and the process of artistic creation that we owe our current assumptions about poetic spontaneity or the expressive character of music. So Wordsworth in the Preface to the *Lyrical Ballads* declared that, 'All good poetry is the spontaneous overflow of powerful feelings'. More than a century later a very different poet, T.S. Eliot, still thought of the artist as expressing emotion as we can see from the way he expounded his concept of the objective correlative:

The only way of expressing emotion in the form of art is by finding an 'objective correlative'; in other words, a set of objects, a situation, a chain of events which shall be the formula of that *particular* emotion; such that when the external facts, which must terminate in sensory experience, are given, the emotion is immediately evoked.[2]

In music performers play a crucial role in transmitting the work to an audience. In a well-known essay first published in 1753 C.P.E. Bach claimed that the performer too must feel the emotions which the music expresses:

A musician cannot move others unless he too is moved. He must of necessity feel all of the affects that he hopes to arouse in his audience . . . In languishing, sad passages the performer must languish and grow sad. Thus will the expression of the piece be more clearly perceived by the audience . . . Similarly, in lively, joyous passages, the executant must again put himself into the appropriate mood . . .[3]

At the same time as practising poets and musicians were for-
mulating such views, expression was becoming increasingly
important in philosophical aesthetics until Croce in his *Aesthetic*,
first published in Italian in 1902, put forward a full-blown theory
of art as expression.

'Expression' has been taken to mean different things by different writers and while some have concentrated on the creative
processes of the artist, others have stressed the evoking of emotion in the audience. I propose to consider here just two variants
of the theory that art is expression: the views of Tolstoy and, at
greater length, the views of Croce and Collingwood. I shall then
return to the problems raised by our common assumption that
works of art express and evoke emotion.

Tolstoy in *What is Art?* presents a simple theory that art is the
contagion of feeling. The true artist both expresses and evokes
emotion. By means of his art he infects his audience with the
feelings he himself experiences. Tolstoy wants to use this theory
as a criterion for the evaluation of art: the quality of art is to be
measured by the quality of the feelings with which it succeeds in
infecting the audience. Thus the art of the wealthy upper classes
which, according to Tolstoy, conveys the feelings of pride, sexual
desire, and discontent with life is regarded as inferior to art with a
wider appeal which conveys more praiseworthy feelings such as
brotherly love. Two other features of this theory are worth noting:
Tolstoy stresses the role of art as communication between the
artist and his audience and he is very concerned to divorce the
appreciation of art from knowledge and intellectual activity. This
second feature accounts for his metaphor of infection and his
insistence that no special learning or training is required to understand what he regards as good art.

When Tolstoy comes to apply his criterion of aesthetic value
the reader is startled to find that he passes sweeping condemnation on almost all of what is normally regarded as art. He condemns not only the operas of Wagner, which he clearly disliked
intensely, but also nearly all his own literary productions. He is
even prepared to deny that Beethoven's Ninth Symphony is good
art, since it does not meet his criterion. Very little is left: Biblical
stories, the *Iliad* and the *Odyssey*, some Indian stories, and a
severely limited selection from modern literature, music, and
visual art. The odd results of applying Tolstoy's criterion of art

should make us suspect that something is wrong with the criterion. A good deal of the trouble comes from the fact that Tolstoy lays down in advance which feelings are worthy to be conveyed by art. Communicating feelings of pride, sexual desire, and discontent with life is regarded as less valuable than communicating brotherly love and the simple feelings of common life. Communicating such feelings may indeed be less valuable on *moral* grounds but so far we have been given no reason to identify moral and aesthetic criteria. Much of Tolstoy's condemnation of art in fact derives from his moral outlook and he fails, or refuses, to make any distinction between the moral and the aesthetic.[4] If we removed the moral element in Tolstoy's theory we would be left with the claim that successful infection of a wide audience is the test of good art. Rock music would score impressively high on this test, a good deal higher than the works of Bach. It is often claimed that a characteristic feature of aesthetic experience is a certain emotional detachment, that in true art emotions are not directly aroused, we are not moved to immediate action but remain in a state of contemplative appreciation.[5] Such a notion of detachment has no place in Tolstoy's theory.

In fact Tolstoy's talk of infection both over-emphasizes and over-simplifies the irrational aspects of our response to art. I would not deny that we can sometimes be deeply moved and fundamentally affected by the experience of art but not all our experience of art is like this and being moved by art is not the same as being moved by events in real life. Having described our response as an infection Tolstoy makes no attempt to analyse it further. The metaphor of infection is even less adequate as a description of what the artist does. Tolstoy talks about the need for the artist to express individual emotions with clarity and sincerity but pays little attention to just how this is done. He claims that if the artist is only sincere, clear expression of individual feeling is bound to follow and successful infection of the audience will be the result.

Tolstoy's view is radical and provocative but its weaknesses and idiosyncrasies are clear enough. It would be difficult to develop his metaphor of infection into a complete theory of the creation of art and our response to it. A much more sophisticated theory of art as expression was put forward by Croce in his *Aesthetic* and developed and amended in a later work, the

Breviary of Aesthetics. In Britain R. G. Collingwood put forward
a theory very close to Croce's in *The Principles of Art.* As the
views of Croce and Collingwood have so much in common I shall
consider them together as one theory.

Both Croce and Collingwood make a fundamental distinction
between conceptual thought on the one hand and on the other
what Croce calls intuition and Collingwood calls imagination.
For Croce intuition means grasping the uniqueness of an object
without classifying it as an object of some particular kind, while
thought involves using concepts to classify and generalize. Both
philosophers divide mental activity into a series of stages, starting
with our reception of the raw data of sensation and perception;
we become properly aware of these at the stage of intuition, or
imagination, when we express them to ourselves and to others.
The formulation of concepts follows at the next stage and beyond
that, in Croce at least, come two further stages in which concepts
are first of all employed to pursue what is useful and then, in the
final stage of mental activity, used for moral ends. This theory,
like Tolstoy's, emphasizes the difference between the creation or
appreciation of art and purely intellectual activity but it attempts,
as Tolstoy's theory does not, to offer an account of just what it is
to express an emotion and how that differs from simply feeling an
emotion.

To understand that account we need to consider more closely
the first three in the series of stages I have just outlined.
Collingwood distinguishes these stages most clearly in Chapter 11
of *The Principles of Art.* I shall broadly follow his exposition and
shall use his terminology. At the first stage, the stage at which we
receive the raw data of sensation and perception, we feel emotions but are somehow not fully conscious of them. We give these
emotions 'psychical expression' when we exhibit the bodily reactions which are their symptoms. So shivering and turning pale are
the psychical expression of fear. These reactions are involuntary,
not subject to our conscious control. They may spread to others
by a process of contagion, as panic spreads involuntarily among a
crowd. Already at this stage a difficulty in the theory becomes
apparent: it is never clearly explained how one can feel an emotion
without being conscious of it. What is clear is that once this
preliminary stage is posited a distinction can be made between the
symptoms of an emotion, its psychical expression, and its

'imaginative expression'. Imaginative expression is expression properly so called. It is the way in which we give voice to our emotions at the second stage, the stage which Collingwood calls imagination and Croce calls intuition. It is at this level that art makes its appearance. Suppose that I am feeling happy. I may walk about with an involuntary smile on my face and sparkling eyes but these reactions are only psychical expression, only symptoms. However, I may also give my happiness imaginative expression: I may sing and dance; I may talk about how happy I feel; if I am an artist I may compose a poem or a piece of music or paint a picture. All these means of expressing my happiness are also means of communicating it to others. Whereas psychical expression simply spreads by involuntary contagion, imaginative expression communicates in a way which requires the conscious attention of a hearer or spectator. To grasp the happiness I am expressing by my singing and dancing others must attend to what I am doing and use their imaginations to recreate my experience for themselves. This is also what they must do if they are to grasp the emotions expressed in a work of art I have made.

We might suppose that when I simply talk about how happy I feel, no such exercise of the imagination by my hearers is required. All they need do is understand the meaning of my words. For Collingwood, however, such understanding of bare meaning belongs to the third stage of mental activity, the stage at which concepts are formulated. If not just the bare meaning of my words but also the 'emotional charge' upon them is to be communicated, my hearers must exercise their imaginations in the same way as they do when they respond to a work of art. Such communication of emotion by means of imaginative expression is to be distinguished from the direct arousal of emotion. My happy singing and dancing or my happy poem will not make my audience happy but will enable them to grasp *my* happiness.

Croce regards intuition and expression as equivalent and is prepared to say either that art is intuition or that art is expression. For Collingwood art is expression at the level of imagination. Both philosophers, having defined art in this way, proceed to treat expression as providing a criterion by which works of art may be evaluated. What is not expression is not art. Thus Collingwood spends a lot of time in *The Principles of Art* condemning various kinds of 'pseudo-art' which are not 'art proper' because they are not pure expression but aim to arouse the audience's emotions for some practical purpose or just for their entertainment. Hymns and patriotic songs are condemned under the first heading, romances and detective stories under the second. Collingwood rules out these kinds of pseudo-art on the grounds that they are crafts which take means to a preconceived end; in true expression the artist does not know what he is expressing until his expression is complete, he cannot see the end result in advance.

It will be evident from my account of the theory so far that Croce and Collingwood concentrate largely on the activity of the artist and on what goes on in his mind. Their theory leads to a paradoxical corollary, that the real work of art is the expression in the artist's mind and that the physical object which we might have taken for the work of art is only its externalization. This view is more plausible for some arts than for others: if I make up a tune, it can indeed exist 'in my head' without being written down and the notes in which I write it down can be thought of as only an aid to my recreating it in my head another time.[6] With a painting on the other hand, its production in the medium of paint on canvas seems all-important. Croce and Collingwood are too quick to generalize over all the arts here. One reason why they do so is that they both subscribed to an idealist metaphysics according to which mental processes are more valuable than material things. Another reason is their stress on art as a way of expressing emotions and intuiting their nature; the sheer hard work of externalizing one's intuition or expression in a physical medium seems to them of secondary importance precisely because it involves technical skill and the deliberate manipulation of means to a given end. They would not deny that expression and externalization might both be going on at the same time, that the painter might come to a full intuitive grasp of what he was trying to paint only as he painted, but they would lay the emphasis firmly on what was happening in the painter's mind, not on what was happening on the canvas.

If the real work of art is in the artist's mind one might suppose that it could never be accessible to an audience. Not so; according to this theory the spectator of visual art, the listener to music, and the reader of literature re-create the artist's expression for themselves. Beethoven's Ninth Symphony as performed is an externalization of Beethoven's intuition; in appreciating it I come to grasp again the intuition that Beethoven grasped, I reproduce his expression in myself.

Summarized like this Croce's and Collingwood's theory may sound absurd. It is open to severe criticism on a number of counts. Yet we can learn from its very failings and an understanding of what Croce and Collingwood were trying to do may help us to appreciate the part played by the emotions in our response to art. In discussing the theory I shall begin with its weakest points.

There is no good reason to accept that the real work of art is in the artist's mind and the account of the audience's response to which that view leads has its own difficulties. Admittedly, Croce and Collingwood are not claiming that the average concert-goer is fully recreating Beethoven's expression when he or she listens to the Ninth Symphony. They recognize that most of us achieve at best a partial recreation of Beethoven's expression. A full grasp of it could be achieved only by mature and experienced listeners, or is perhaps no more than an ideal to which we all strive but which none of us realize. Once we allow for such development in the audience's response to art, Croce's and Collingwood's account of that response gains in plausibility. We can come back to great works of art time and time again and feel that we are gradually growing in understanding of them. Nevertheless, to regard such a growth in understanding as a gradual approximation to what went on in the mind of the artist does not really help us to comprehend this feature of our experience. For one thing, we shall quickly have to allow that the artist's mind may contain elements of which he is unconscious since it is common for the audience of a work of art to find in it features the artist did not consciously put there. For another, the diversity of interpretations and reactions creates a difficulty. Suppose two listeners agree that Beethoven's Ninth is a great musical work, agree also on which formal features of it they find particularly impressive but give differing accounts of the emotions they take Beethoven to have been expressing in it. Which of them has successfully grasped Beethoven's intuition? If we say that one of them is right and the other is wrong, how do we show that to be so? Consideration of this case brings us to the real difficulty here: there is no way of checking what Beethoven's intuition was other than by listening to the music. If he had left a detailed account in words of what he was trying to express that would not help us, for he might have expressed more in the music than he consciously intended to and Croce himself would say that the account in words was at a different level, the level of conceptual thought, and so was not a reliable guide to the artistic expression or intuition. But if we cannot know the artist's expression except through the work, it is misleading to maintain that what was in the artist's mind is more real or more valuable than the object he has produced.[7]

Admittedly in the case of music and literature we cannot find one physical object which we can call the work of art, as we can with painting, sculpture, or architecture. Beethoven's Ninth is not identical with any one copy of the score or any one recording. If some copies of T.S. Eliot's *The Waste Land* were destroyed in a fire, the poem itself would be undamaged for the poem is not identical with any one copy of the text. Recognition of this fact, however, does not afford sufficient reason for saying that Beethoven's Ninth was really in his mind and is re-created by experienced listeners or that in learning to appreciate *The Waste Land* we are learning to reproduce in ourselves precisely what went on in Eliot's mind when he wrote it.

Another difficulty in Croce's and Collingwood's theory is their neglect of the differences between the arts. They both denied that there were any significant differences between literary genres or between literature and the other arts. Such a denial follows from their view that the true work of art is in the artist's mind and that its externalization in a particular physical medium is a secondary matter, but it runs counter to the reality of aesthetic experience. Poems, paintings, and pieces of music are very different sorts of thing—as we have seen, paintings are physical objects as poems and pieces of music are not—and we respond to them in different ways, using different kinds of critical vocabulary. At the same time these differences are not so great as to make it impossible to utter any general remarks at all about works of art and our experiences of them. A frequent source of difficulties in aesthetics is the tension between the diversity of art and our sense that works of art do share common features. Croce and Collingwood fail to do justice to this tension.

Finally, as with Tolstoy's theory, the results of applying Croce's and Collingwood's theory in practice are rather alarming. Collingwood in particular regards only a very limited range of works as 'art proper'. The works of Dante, T.S. Eliot, Yeats, Jane Austen, Cézanne, and Mozart are admitted to the canon, together with some of Beethoven and a few plays of Shakespeare. Not much else passes the test. What is worse, it is not even clear how the test is to be applied. At least on Tolstoy's theory we could go round and see how many people had been infected and with what sort of emotions. But what are the criteria for determining whether what purports to be art is expression and so 'art proper'? They seem to be largely negative: the work must not do anything so vulgar as arouse emotion directly or have any ulterior purpose. After that we have to fall back on a judgement of what was going on in the artist's mind and what goes on in the minds of an audience. All we can do is examine our own reactions to the work introspectively, to see if they are in some measure a re-creating of the artist's expression. Yet since we do not have access to the artist's mind, it is impossible to tell whether we have grasped his expression successfully. Once again the emphasis this theory lays on rather mysterious processes in the mind leads to difficulties.

Despite its weaknesses, Croce's and Collingwood's theory should not just be dismissed as an extravagant fantasy. It is worth considering a little more closely just what the theory was trying to do. Like Tolstoy, Croce and Collingwood wished to give due weight to the differences between art and conceptual thought, to the fact that creating a work of art is not a purely intellectual activity, nor is aesthetic appreciation the same as intellectual understanding.[8] At the same time they wished to avoid the mistake of identifying the production of art with displaying symptoms of emotion and aesthetic response with the direct arousal of emotion. There is something wrong with the spectator at a performance of *Othello* who sits there with a polite smile on his face and at the end merely says, 'Well, that was a strange story. What about a drink?' We expect the spectator to become more involved with the play, to be in some sense emotionally affected by it, to display not only an intellectual interest in following the story but also some emotional concern with the characters. The spectator who simply does not care is not responding to the play as art at all. Yet something is equally wrong with the spectator who becomes too directly involved and reacts as though he were seeing a real murder enacted on the stage, who leaps from his seat crying, 'No! Don't do it!' and who bursts into tears when his attempts to restrain Othello are unheeded. Being moved by a play is not the same as being moved by a situation in real life.

Aesthetic theory must walk a tightrope between over-intellectualizing the response to art and assimilating the response too closely to the emotional responses of real life. One of the defects of the view that art is imitation, discussed in the previous chapter, is that it can make the response to art too intellectual. It may be true, as Aristotle said, that we take pleasure in recognizing that one thing is an imitation of another[9] but this is not the whole story about aesthetic pleasure. Tolstoy's talk of infection, on the other hand, makes little distinction between the role of the emotions in aesthetic appreciation and the role of the emotions in everyday life. Croce and Collingwood are attempting to walk this tightrope, to explain how the production of art and the response to it differ both from purely intellectual activities and from immediate emotional reactions.

In the end Croce and Collingwood fail because they concentrate too much on what they take to be going on in the mind of the creative artist and because they exaggerate the importance of their notion of expression. They do too little justice to the intellectual elements in art and to the fact that art can arouse some sorts of emotion directly. Art may not be all craft but craft plays a considerable part in it. To appreciate Catullus' poetry to the full one needs to recognize his technical skill as well as respond to the emotions he is expressing. A successful work of art may arouse some emotions, express others, and exhibit technical mastery, all at the same time. A play like Molière's *Tartuffe* arouses amusement and makes us laugh but our laughter does not prevent us from responding to the anger at hypocrisy which is being expressed or from recognizing Molière's skill as a dramatist.

Whatever the strengths and weaknesses of particular variants of the view that art is expression, in the end they all founder in the same way that theories of art as imitation founder. Expression is only one aspect of art. Some works are more expressive than others and there is more than just expression to even the most expressive works. We may think more readily in terms of the composer expressing emotions when we listen to Mahler than when we listen to Bach but it would be foolish to regard Mahler as lacking in technical skill or to claim that his music could not be analysed in formal terms.

If we admit the importance of expression in the production of art and in our appreciation of it, without going so far as to claim that all art is expression and nothing else, we still require to give some account of what is meant by talking about art as expressing emotions. We have seen that there are difficulties in the way of interpreting such talk as being simply about the artist putting his emotions into the work. We cannot know what those emotions were, except from the work, and it would be much too crude to assume that only a sad composer can produce sad music, only a poet in love can write love poetry, only an angry painter can produce an angry painting. We have to be careful here to do justice to the diversity of art and the diversity of artists. If not all love poetry is written by people who are passionately in love, it does not follow that no love poetry is written by real lovers. The difficulty is that often we cannot know how closely the emotions expressed in the work of art correspond to the emotions felt by the artist. Since our interest is in any case in the work rather than its maker, it is prudent to talk about the emotions expressed in the work without making too many biographical inferences about the artist.

Nevertheless, it is often quite hard to put this critical principle into practice and we may well wonder what is meant by talking about emotions 'in' the work. Love poetry is poetry that purports to be written by someone who is in love and which makes it possible for us to imagine what it is like to be such a person, whether or not we are in love ourselves. What then of sad music? We might suppose it more plausible to regard this as music which makes the listener feel sad rather than as music which purports to be composed by a sad person. Yet it does not make us feel sad in the way in which news of the death of someone we know makes us feel sad.[10] Perhaps rather it makes us imagine what it is like to feel sad, or makes us feel sad in some special, detached, aesthetic kind of way. There are two problems here. One is whether there are certain qualities in works of art which can be objectively defined and which are always describable in terms of certain emotions: are minor keys in music, for instance, always plaintive and if so, why? The other problem is just what is meant by 'imagining what it is like to feel so-and-so' or 'feeling so-and-so in a special, detached, aesthetic kind of way'.

One class of terms quite often used of works of art raises the first problem but not the second. Terms such as 'disturbing', 'amusing', 'terrifying', 'entertaining' refer straightforwardly to the arousal of emotion. If I say that the paintings of Hieronymus Bosch are disturbing, I mean in the first instance that something about them disturbs me and I claim implicitly that they will disturb others too. If I say that *Tartuffe* is an amusing play I mean that it arouses amusement in me, it makes me laugh, and I am claiming it will have that effect on others too. We may still ask, however, just what it is about a painting that makes it disturbing or about a play that makes it amusing. Are there certain features that always make paintings disturbing or plays amusing?

Several writers have suggested that our fundamental model for attributing expressive properties to things is the way the human body and the human face look and behave.[11] Sad music, it is said, is music which sounds like sad people, people who move slowly and speak in low voices. I doubt, however, whether such an approach will account for all the expressive qualities we find in art. It may work for simple attributions like 'sad' but will it work for more subtle ones such as 'plaintive', 'melancholy', 'serene', or 'optimistic'? It is not even clear that it works for 'sad'. Some sad people move slowly and speak in low voices but others move more brusquely than usual and speak in harsh tones. Still others move and speak as normal but betray their sadness by the look on their faces or the posture of their limbs. Yet we are probably more inclined to say that slow, soft music is sad than that brusque, harsh music is so. Sad music cannot of course look like a sad face; we might suppose that a sad abstract painting would do this but I am not sure that it would. A sad abstract painting might well be one in 'sad' colours, blues, browns, and greys—but then what makes sad colours sad?

In part the question why we associate particular expressive properties with particular works of art is a psychological question. It may well be that analogies with human behaviour and the expression of the human face explain some of the associations that we make between, for example, soft, slow music and sadness. Although not all sad people move slowly or speak in low voices, this is one of the commonest ways in which human beings express sadness and so it is treated as the norm which provides the analogy. Other kinds of association may also be at work. Green is a colour that people find restful and this might mean that we found a green abstract painting calm and restful and described it as such. If we ask why we find green restful, we enter the realm of psychological rather than philosophical speculation. A disturbing painting might be one in which a variety of shapes were jumbled together without any apparent plan. Why we find a jumbled mass of shapes disturbing is again a psychological question. If we ask what makes a situation amusing we shall find that a great deal of comedy involves some kind of reversal of our expectations about what is to happen or what will be said. That we find such a reversal funny is a psychological fact about human beings.

The behavioural and facial expression of emotion differs in some respects from one culture to another and cultural factors may also be responsible for the association of particular expressive properties with particular works of art. In Indian music there are different ragas for different times of day but to a Western ear it is far from obvious why one kind of raga is associated with the morning and another with the evening.

However, when we are concerned with particular works of art we should not expect to find that our attribution of expressive qualities to them can only be supported in such general psychological or cultural terms. In explaining what is disturbing about a painting by Hieronymus Bosch we may want to pick out figures or groups of figures in one particular painting rather than generalize about the psychological effects of Bosch's art. In explaining what is amusing about *Tartuffe* we may want to draw attention to individual scenes rather than concern ourselves with the nature of comedy in general. To learn to appreciate a piece of Indian music it may be just as important to listen carefully to particular passages as to learn about Indian attitudes to music. Criticism of an individual work of art may involve explaining precisely why we find certain expressive qualities in it and this may mean appealing to specific features of the work as well as to general psychological and cultural associations.

The search for definitions of particular expressive properties in works of art leads us either into psychology or into criticism and away from philosophy as such. Can any progress be made towards giving a philosophical account of our response to such properties, when it is not simply the arousal of emotion? What is the difference between feeling an emotion in the ordinary way and feeling an emotion as we do when contemplating a work of art which displays certain emotional qualities, between the way we feel when we hear of the death of someone we know and the way we feel when we hear sad music? Imagination plays a part here just as it does in our response to representation. I suggested earlier that love poetry makes us imagine what it feels like to be in love. This, however, is a case where expression and representation go together. Catullus in his Lesbia poems is both expressing the feeling of being in love and offering a representation of a man in love which is akin to a representation in a play. Similarly, John Donne in 'The Sunne Rising' expresses his feelings for his beloved by representing himself as addressing the morning sun which breaks in upon the lovers. The dramatic opening of the poem immediately assists us in imagining the situation:

> Busie old foole, unruly Sunne,
> Why dost thou thus,
> Through windows and through curtains call on us?
> Must to thy motions lovers seasons run?

In literature expression and representation often go together in this kind of way and we may be helped to an understanding of what is being expressed by our recognition of what is being represented. The same is true of representational painting. If we look at Uccello's painting, *The Battle of San Romano*, the very knowledge that what is represented is a battle limits the range of emotions we might expect to find expressed in it (see Plate 2). We may look in it for triumph, or for grief, but not for light-hearted jollity. It might be easier to isolate what is involved in responding to expression if we confined our attention to music, which is seldom representational. Sometimes the title of a piece of music indicates what we should expect to find expressed in it. If we know a piece is entitled 'Funeral March' we shall start thinking of funerals and the grief associated with them. But what do we experience when we respond to sadness in music without being given any such cue by a title? Are we imagining what it is like to feel sad? Or are we feeling sad in some peculiar detached way, or feeling something akin to sadness which yet is not sadness?

Part of the problem here lies in the difficulty of giving a satisfactory philosophical account of emotion. Before we can say what it is to feel sad in some peculiar detached way, we need to be able to say what it is to feel sad in the ordinary way. At one level we all know perfectly well from introspection what feeling sad is like and when we think someone else is feeling sad we are inferring from their behaviour—their movements, their tone of voice, the look on their face—that they are feeling the emotion we are familiar with from our own experience. The difficulty lies in proceeding beyond this to some general account of the nature of sadness, given in terms on which others will agree. Such an account would enable us not only to describe sadness but to distinguish it from related emotions such as gloom and melancholy. There are three lines of approach which might be tried. One is to pick out the typical objects of an emotion. The object of an emotion is the person, thing, or situation towards which it is directed. When asked to give the reason for an emotion, we normally refer to its object. Thus, if I am sad at my aunt's death, my aunt's death is the object of my sadness and I will refer to it when asked why I am sad. Typical objects of sadness would be bereavement, loss, and disappointment. Another line of approach, already alluded to, is to pick out the characteristic behaviour or types of behaviour displayed by sad people, the movements, the tone of voice, the look on the face, the posture of the limbs. In this area in particular we shall have to be wary of falling into circularity and simply saying that the characteristic look on a sad person's face is an expression of sadness. We shall have to speak of a mouth which does not smile or of eyes which do not sparkle and endeavour to keep away from language which appeals to the emotional state which we take the behaviour or the look to express. It will not be easy. The third line of approach is to describe one's own feelings as accurately as possible using introspection. This too is difficult. In describing emotional states we readily resort to metaphor—'I felt waves of gloom sweeping over me'—or to appeals to the way other people feel in comparable situations—'I felt the way you might feel if you had applied for fifty jobs and failed to get an interview for any of them'. Such descriptions can be perfectly comprehensible but require the hearers in turn to use their imaginations to try to feel for themselves what we are feeling.

Exactly what should be classed as 'emotions' is not altogether clear and this too makes it difficult to give a lucid account of emotion. As well as trying to determine the objects, the behaviour, and the experiences characteristic of particular emotions, a philosophical account of the emotions would have to discriminate between different kinds of affective states, for example between moods such as depression or elation and emotions such as grief or anger. While moods have no specific object but colour our reactions and our general behaviour for as long as they last, emotions do normally have an object and are expressed in some characteristic behaviour rather than colouring all that we do. Thus if I am depressed there may be no particular reason for it and I may go around with my shoulders hunched and without a smile and fail to take much interest in anything. If I am stricken with grief, on the other hand, there will be a reason for it, such as a bereavement, and I am likely to do specific things such as cry and find it hard to speak of the person who has died.

The line between moods and emotions can be hard to draw. In particular, such common emotion-terms as 'sadness' and 'happiness' are used sometimes of moods and sometimes of emotions. Easier to distinguish are sensations which are physically located in some part of the body, such as aches, tingles, and itches. These are often discussed in the context of emotion since they may be associated with emotions and moods or give rise to them or be caused by them. A headache, for example, may be either a symptom or a cause or an effect of a mood of depression. However, such physically locatable sensations belong on the margin of an account of emotion rather than at the centre.

It would take quite a time to complete a proper study of emotion in this kind of way. If at the end of such a long journey we returned to the way we respond to emotions expressed in works of art, what would we find? I have two suggestions here for the way the enquiry might proceed. First, we saw that in trying to describe our experience of an emotion we often fall back on metaphor or on appeals to the way other people feel in comparable situations, and that such descriptions in turn require our hearers to use their imaginations. It is not just a matter of saying, 'Imagine what it is like to feel sad', for to that we might well retort, 'Sad about what? I can't just feel sad in the abstract'. Rather we are saying, 'Imagine how you would feel if the fiftieth letter of rejection had just arrived'. We are asking our hearers to imagine a situation and their imagined emotion, if that is what it is, will arise out of that. This in turn leads to my second point, that the very nature of emotional response to works of art drives us away from general theory and back towards a study of particular works. A representational work of art, at least, presents us with a situation in which we are to imagine how *we* would feel. It is hard to imagine emotions without any situation being set up in which to do so. Perhaps the way forward lies in a sensitive study of responses to individual works of art and attempts at generalization should only follow such a study.

We have still not solved the problem presented by abstract arts such as music which seem to express emotions but do *not* present us with a situation in which to imagine how we would feel. And it remains unclear what it is to imagine feeling an emotion and how that is related to feeling the emotion in some special, detached way. Let us take the first problem first. An expressive piece of music sometimes stimulates us to imagine a situation for ourselves. Whereas in representational art we are given the situation and asked to imagine feeling the emotion, in music we are presented with a stimulus to the emotion and in imagining feeling the emotion we may imagine a situation too. This is why we have an urge to relate the emotion we find in the music to a situation in the composer's life. We want to make the emotion into a recognizable one which arises out of a particular situation. But what kind of stimulus to the emotion are we being given? The stimulus may take different forms with different pieces of music. Sometimes the music may suggest the typical objects of an emotion: at the crudest level a sudden roll on the drums which sounds like thunder may evoke fear, although we know there is nothing really to be afraid of. Sometimes the music may suggest behaviour characteristic of someone who is experiencing the emotion: we are back with the slow movement and the soft sound again. Or sometimes there may be some kind of correspondence with the way we ourselves feel when we experience the emotion so that we would use the same metaphor in attempting to describe it: music may be said to ripple or flow, for instance, and so may emotions.[12] This last kind of link is the hardest to make sense of and yet is something we experience quite frequently in listening to music.

An example may be helpful here. Mozart's Clarinet Concerto strikes the listener as a happy, cheerful piece. It was written towards the end of Mozart's life and completed not long before his death, at the same time as he was writing his *Requiem*, in poverty and poor health. The music does not sound like any typical objects of happiness. Parts of the first and third movements suggest in their rhythms the behaviour of happy people skipping and dancing but this by itself does not provide an adequate account of how the concerto expresses happiness. We may come closer to understanding what makes this a happy piece if we attend to such features as the tone of the clarinet, the part it plays in relation to the other instruments, and the musical intervals used. These features somehow remind us of the way we feel when we feel happy, they make us imagine feeling happy, or indeed they may arouse actual emotions of happiness. But 'the way we feel when we feel happy' is not readily described and it is difficult to analyse in general terms just what features of music regularly correspond to that feeling. In explaining why we call Mozart's Clarinet Concerto a happy piece we will be more successful if we point to particular passages and say, 'Listen to the sound of the clarinet here' than if we devise some general description of the characteristics of happy music. Once again we have reached a point where progress requires the careful study of individual works.

I turn now to the second problem. What is it to imagine feeling an emotion? It might be that there are different kinds of such imagining, of which one in particular may also be described as feeling the emotion in the detached way appropriate to art. I alluded at the beginning of this chapter to Wordsworth's claim in the Preface to the *Lyrical Ballads* that, 'All good poetry is the spontaneous overflow of powerful feelings'. Wordsworth also said there that poetry 'takes its origin from emotion recollected in tranquillity', suggesting that for the poet too a certain detachment is required. We shall consider this detachment further in Chapter 5 and that will help to clarify how the response to art differs from other kinds of imagining emotion.[13] First, though, we should examine an important aspect of works of art hitherto mentioned only in passing.

The hardest case for the understanding of expression proved to be music. We saw that it is difficult to say precisely how music, which for the most part is not representational but has purely formal qualities, can express emotions. When we try to pick out which features of Mozart's Clarinet Concerto make it a happy piece, we in fact draw attention to formal features of the work such as the rhythms and the musical intervals. It is the formal features of musical works which suggest the typical objects of an emotion, remind us of the behaviour characteristic of someone who experiences the emotion, or somehow correspond with the way we ourselves feel when we experience the emotion. Form in art deserves more detailed discussion and will be the subject of the next chapter.

4

Form

Critical descriptions of works of music tend to be couched either in terms of the emotions expressed—'After a serene and joyful opening the music becomes progressively more disturbed and anguished until at last it issues in a final outburst of grief'—or in terms of the formal features of the piece—'The work opens in C major but then changes into a minor key; the theme introduced by the oboe is taken up by the violins; the rhythms become increasingly syncopated . . .'—or, often, in some combination of these two vocabularies. A description in terms of formal features will be more precise and is more likely to appeal to experienced and knowledgeable listeners who can follow the work in these terms. The ability to pick out the formal features of a piece of music leads to a heightened appreciation of it, and experienced listeners will value highly works whose formal qualities they particularly admire. Of all the arts, music is the one in which formal qualities are most important and most readily perceived. Yet they are a source of aesthetic value in the other arts too. In ballet, for example, we find beauty in the formal patterns made by the movements of the dancers.

In visual art formal qualities are a good deal more important than a naïve spectator might at first suppose. Greek sculpture of the classical period, for instance, is often admired for its command of the proportions of the human figure; the balance achieved is very pleasing to the eye. The *Doryphoros* ('Spearbearer') of Polykleitos, one of the most celebrated of all classical Greek statues, was treated by subsequent generations of artists as a model for harmonious proportion.[1] The Renaissance architect Palladio modelled his buildings on principles of symmetry and proportion[2] and a concern for formal balance in composition can be seen in many Renaissance paintings. Uccello's *The Battle of San Romano* is only one of the most striking examples. In modern abstract paintings such as those of Ben Nicholson form has become all-important.

In literature, too, formal qualities may help to explain why we value particular works. In this case the range of features which count as 'formal' is exceedingly wide. The metre used for verse, the ordering of words, and the structure of a plot are all matters of form. The range and variety of formal features in literature will become clear if we consider some examples. Gerard Manley Hopkins's use of an idiosyncratic 'sprung rhythm' for his poetry is a formal feature which makes his work distinctive, while the arrangement and rhythm of the words contribute to the impressive effect made by the Authorized Version of the Bible. On another level of form, the interweaving of plot and sub-plots is fundamental to the structure of many novels by Dickens and Trollope. Even the arrangement of themes in a play, a novel, or a poem may be regarded as a formal feature. The three linked plays which make up Aeschylus' *Oresteia* are all concerned with the same theme, justice, and the presentation of this theme from different points of view shapes the trilogy and gives it a greater coherence than would be given by the plot alone.

Reflection on my examples from music and visual art will make it plain that here too 'form' covers a host of different things. In visual art 'formal features' include not only balance and symmetry but also perspective. Normally these are all produced by the arrangement of shapes and lines. In some paintings, those of Titian for example, contrasting colours, rather than shapes, are used to produce effects of symmetry and balance and so there is a case for including colour too among the formal features of painting. In music 'formal features' can include the key chosen, the rhythms, the role of different instruments, and the intervals between notes.

Despite the diversity of what counts as 'formal', there is one thing which all these examples have in common: in every case relationships between features are involved. In visual art the relationships may be between shapes or between colours; in music they may be between notes or between instruments; in literature they may be between metrical units, words, parts of a plot, or presentations of a theme. In every case it is the ordering of the formal features which matters.

Much criticism of the arts has stressed the importance of form, concentrated on the formal qualities of works, and sometimes even denied that any other qualities are aesthetically relevant. In literature both the American New Critics, such as Cleanth Brooks, and the French structuralists, notably Roland Barthes, are in different ways formalists. The structuralists explicitly acknowledge their debts to the Russian Formalists of the beginning of this century.[3] The development of these trends in literary criticism has followed on an increased concern with form on the part of literary artists. It is significant that some of the most successful work of the French structuralist critic, Tzvetan Todorov, discusses the thematic structure of Henry James's short stories, for James is a highly self-conscious writer much concerned with form. Todorov sees the central feature of the Jamesian short story as a quest for an essentially absent secret and he is able to support this interpretation of James by appealing to James's own story, *The Figure in the Carpet*, which traces the search by a young critic for the secret which informs an admired author's work; the reader of the story never discovers what this secret is.[4] The structuralists in their turn have been followed and criticized from the inside by writers such as Jacques Derrida. Derrida's method of 'deconstruction', of exposing the internal contradictions in a literary or philosophical text, remains very much concerned with the formal features of the text under consideration.[5] In a number of these formalist critics their critical practice is accompanied, or even overshadowed, by a theoretical view that it is the forms and structures of literary works which make them what they are and that literary study is essentially the study of such forms and structures.

A similar concern with form developed in the criticism and theory of music and of visual art in the second half of the nineteenth century and the first half of the twentieth. In music the Viennese critic Eduard Hanslick not only stressed formal qualities in his criticism but wrote what has become a classic of musical aesthetics, *The Beautiful in Music*, arguing that the beauty of music was to be found in its formal qualities. In the visual arts it was two practising art critics, Clive Bell and Roger Fry, who developed the theory that the essential quality of art was what they called 'significant form' and their concern with the formal qualities of art can be seen clearly in their criticism.

The theory that the essence of art is to be found in form is the third general type of theory about art which we shall consider. Historically modern theories of art as form developed out of expressionist theories of the kind considered in the previous chapter and a number of formalist theories retain elements of expressionism, as we shall see. A search for expression or expressiveness 'in' a work of art leads easily to a close concern with the details of the work itself, including its form and structure. We saw at the end of the last chapter how this was especially true of music. In fact any type of criticism which takes a work of art in itself, not the maker or the audience, as its primary concern and studies the way the work is put together, will be to some extent concerned with formal features of a work.

A strong interest in artistic form is already evident not only in classical art and literature but also in ancient literary criticism and aesthetic theory. Although Aristotle's overall theory in the *Poetics* is a distinctive version of the view that art is imitation, when he discusses tragedy and epic in detail he deals mainly with their formal features. In the eighteenth century Kant in his *Critique of Aesthetic Judgement* made a distinction between 'free' and 'dependent' beauty and claimed that free beauty is ascribed to an object in virtue of its form alone, without consideration of any end to which the object may be directed. He offered flowers and patterns of intertwining lines on wallpaper as examples of free beauty.[6] Kant's views have had a pervasive influence on subsequent aesthetic theory and it is Kant's account of beauty as form which directly or indirectly lies behind a number of later formalist accounts of art.

I propose to pick out two of the formalist theories already mentioned for discussion. I shall consider first the formalist view of music espoused by Hanslick and second the view of visual art as significant form put forward by Clive Bell and Roger Fry. As a pendant I shall examine the way certain aspects of this second view are developed by Susanne Langer. Neither of the two theories I shall discuss is concerned with art in general. In considering whether such theories could be extended to cover all the arts, and in particular how they could give an account of literature, we shall reach some general conclusions about the nature of formalist aesthetic theories and their value.

In *The Beautiful in Music* Hanslick argues that a proper aesthetic contemplation of music involves only the music itself, considered for its own sake and without reference to any further end. What is thus contemplated is the sounds of the music and the forms created by their movement, namely the melody, the harmony, the rhythm, and the instrumentation. According to Hanslick, it is such elements which the composer has in mind when he composes a piece of music; the composer thinks of his piece in purely musical terms and the listener should do likewise. In listening to a piece of music we derive satisfaction from following and anticipating the movement of the sounds, from attending to the formal pattern of the music.

Hanslick presents his case attractively and at first sight it seems persuasive. Yet his view is limited in a number of ways. First, it should be noted that Hanslick confines his argument entirely to music, the art of which he was a practising critic. This helps to give strength to his position, for of all the arts music is the one where formal features are most clearly dominant. Secondly, Hanslick's arguments are largely negative ones. In particular he argues against the idea that music can represent anything or can express specific emotions. He admits that music may arouse particular feelings in the hearer but regards this as a secondary and not purely aesthetic effect. He also allows that music can represent what he calls 'the dynamic properties of feelings', that is, those properties which are associated with audible changes in strength, speed, and the intervals between notes. So he says, 'Music may reproduce phenomena such as whispering, storming, roaring but the feelings of love or anger have only a subjective existence. Definite feelings and emotions are unsusceptible of being embodied in music', and he refers more generally to the capacity of music to express 'the ideas of intensity waxing and diminishing; of motion hastening and lingering; of ingeniously complex and simple progression, etc.'.[7] This is the view, mentioned in the previous chapter, that we use expressive language to describe music because there is some kind of correspondence between the music and the way we feel when we experience a particular emotion. Hanslick would say there is a correspondence between the movement of the music and the movement of our feelings and that this is the only way in which music can express emotions.

This is only a limited concession to the expressive element in music, for while Hanslick might grant that a piece of music which had beauty of form was also expressive he denies that the expressive quality contributes to the beauty. For beauty in music only the formal pattern matters. Moreover, he does not push very far his analysis of how music can be expressive. As we saw in the previous chapter it is in fact difficult to offer a detailed analysis of how music is expressive in Hanslick's sense; such a view cannot really be explained except by considering individual cases.

Sometimes a piece of music can be given a more specific expressive content by its title, or by words of a song which may be set to it. Schubert's 'Death and the Maiden' Quartet, for example, is so called because the second, slow movement is a set of variations on a song with that title. If we listen to the quartet as a whole without thinking of the title it does not sound particularly sad, but the title tempts the listener to find sadness in the music and the work has even been interpreted as a premonition of death. Hanslick does consider such cases but dismisses them. He deliberately excludes from his discussion not only pieces in which words are set to music but programme music and pieces with specific titles, regarding instrumental music alone as 'pure and self-subsistent music'.[8] This introduces an element of circularity into his position: he considers only music in which form is supremely important and then concludes that only form matters for determining the beauty of a piece of music. The exclusion, modest as it may seem at first, in fact cuts out a great deal of music without independent justification. Hanslick's theory is meant to apply only over a very narrow field: it is limited not just to music, but to purely instrumental music.

Since he excludes music to which words are set it is not surprising that Hanslick is distinctly suspicious of the mixed art of opera. In his view opera, as a combination of drama and music, entails 'perpetual warfare' between the two arts which are being combined so that it can never be as successful as either of these arts on its own.[9] It would certainly be a mistake to judge an opera by exactly the same criteria as those by which we judge either an independent piece of music or a play but Hanslick is going further than this and denying that opera can succeed by *any* criteria. Hanslick's suspicion of combining the 'pure' art of music with any other and even of contaminating music by a specific title is, as we shall see, characteristic of formalism. To maintain that any art is essentially formal usually entails a preference for examples that are as purely formal as possible and so are particularly favourable to the theory. In fact the case is the same as with the other types of general aesthetic theory we have already considered: Hanslick's theory does not do full justice to the diversity of art. He makes no claims to consider all the arts and his fault lies not in failing to do that but in not doing justice even to the diversity of his chosen art, music. To exclude opera is reasonable and to exclude music accompanied by words may be justifiable but it is simply arbitrary to exclude all programme music and all pieces with titles which suggest a specific reference. Hanslick gives too little consideration to the way in which the formal structure and the expressive or representational elements are related in the types of music he excludes. Nevertheless, his treatment of form in music does pick out the significant formal features and his account is persuasive for some music, if not for all. Perhaps he would say this was all he wished to achieve.

A similar view with reference to visual art was put forward independently of Hanslick by Clive Bell and Roger Fry. It was Bell in his book *Art* who introduced the phrase 'significant form' and claimed that this and this alone was the distinctive characteristic of great art which aroused a special 'aesthetic emotion'. Bell introduced his theory as part of a crusade to persuade the public to be more sympathetic to Post-Impressionist painting and he saw Cézanne as the prime example of a painter whose paintings had significant form. In Part III of *Art* he presents his own idiosyncratic view of the development of Western art. According to Bell archaic Greek art and medieval art deserve high praise while classical Greek art and the art of the Renaissance, impressive as they are, exhibit a decline in the ability to create significant form. This ability was rediscovered by Cézanne and the Post-Impressionists. The reason why Bell values classical Greek art and Renaissance art less highly than the art of the immediately preceding periods is instructive. He disapproves of the interest in realistic imitation displayed in the classical period of Greek art and in the Renaissance. Like Hanslick's, Bell's arguments for his own views are largely negative arguments against another theory, in this case the theory that what matters in visual art is accuracy of representation. He values the Post-Impressionist readiness to sacrifice realistic imitation in the pursuit of other artistic aims.

While Hanslick argues that only pure instrumental music deserves consideration, Bell is primarily concerned with paintings by only one group of painters, the Post-Impressionists, although in his sketch of the history of Western art he does try to fit other schools of painting into the strait-jacket of his theory. If Bell's theory is less convincing than Hanslick's on first reading it is in part because his favoured range of examples is so much more obviously restricted.

Roger Fry shared Clive Bell's enthusiasm for the Post-Impressionists and in his theoretical writings on art he upheld a position similar to Clive Bell's in that he argued against regarding representation as supremely important in visual art and stressed the importance of form and structural design. At the same time he criticized Bell for taking his theory too far and his own writings display a greater flexibility of approach and a greater awareness of the diverse ways in which visual art can succeed.[10]

In both Bell and Fry the importance of form in visual art is constantly reiterated rather than developed into a full-blown theory. Bell never really explains what sort of form counts as significant and both Bell and Fry talk of a special aesthetic emotion aroused by the perception of significant form but do not define or analyse it.

In considering this view two difficulties must be discussed. First, while it is not difficult to isolate the formal elements in music as Hanslick would have us do, it is much less clear that the formal features of visual art can be considered in isolation. Secondly, talk of significant form naturally provokes the question, 'significant of what?' Bell did indeed attempt to answer this question but as we shall see his answer is far from satisfactory.

Consider again Uccello's painting, *The Battle of San Romano*. The painting is carefully balanced. In the foreground are two groups of fighters, the victorious group on the left larger than the routed group on the right, while in the background the right-hand side of the picture is the one which contains figures and interest. The horses' raised legs are drawn in an angular way which emphasizes their shape and the fallen weapons and helmets on the ground are arranged in an almost mathematical pattern. Here is a painting in which formal features are clearly very important. Yet it would be difficult to describe the shapes in the painting without saying what they are shapes *of* and it would be even more difficult to see them just as shapes. The pattern at the bottom of the painting is not just a pattern of brown and yellow lines and blobs on a pinkish-brown surface but a pattern of weapons and helmets lying on the ground. The two thick, bent white lines beside the brown and yellow ones are not just lines attached to the white blob above them but the shape made by the hind legs of a horse as it rears up.

It might be thought that this difficulty is simply a matter of inexperience, that we could, and indeed should, accustom ourselves to seeing such a painting as this purely in terms of coloured shapes and lines. The difficulty, however, goes deeper than one might at first suppose. In seeing the thick, bent white lines as the legs of a rearing horse we are seeing them as moving three-dimensional objects although in fact they have only two dimensions and are not moving at all. If we are to look at this painting in purely formal terms we shall have to abstract its shapes not only from the things they represent but also from any notions of movement or depth in space. Thus the slanting lines on the left of the picture which represent the pikes of the victorious army as it advances are not slanting some to the right and some to the left just to make a pretty pattern. The ones which look as if they are in front are slanting to the right because they are meant to be moving in the same direction as the army itself. That slant, together with the larger size of the group of warriors on the left, helps to create the impression that the army on the left is gaining the upper hand, and even if we manage to see the pikes just as lines slanting forward we will still tend to see them as moving to the right. If we were seeing them in purely formal terms we should do nothing of the kind. It is still harder not to see the forms in a painting as three-dimensional. I spoke cautiously of slanting lines which 'look as if they are in front' and alluded earlier to the foreground and background of the painting. This painting by Uccello is less sophisticated in its use of the techniques of perspective than many later Renaissance paintings, and yet it is almost impossible not to see the smaller lines of pikes as behind the larger ones or to regard the small figures in the top right-hand corner as being in the background. Canvases are in two dimensions while paintings are usually of things in three dimensions and in the recognition of a painted shape as three-dimensional some minimal element of representation is already creeping in.[11]

In abstract paintings we do find just shapes and colours but even there one shape may appear to be behind another or shapes may seem to be moving across a picture. Moreover Cézanne and

the other Post-Impressionist painters whom Bell and Fry wished
to defend were not abstract painters. The forms in a Cézanne
painting are as much forms *of* something as the forms in an
Uccello painting. The point is not just that it is difficult to describe
many paintings in purely formal terms; that can usually be done
if we try hard enough. Rather, the crux of the matter is that psychologically it is almost impossible actually to see a painting in
that way. Indeed, our natural tendency is to see representation
where there is none, so hard do we find it to consider visual forms
in total isolation.

Nevertheless, suppose that we could train ourselves to see
paintings purely and simply as patterns of two-dimensional
forms. The result would be that most of them would cease to hold
much interest for us. The use of form in Uccello's painting is
interesting precisely because he has represented in a very ordered
way what would in reality be a chaotic scene. We should take
much less interest in the picture if it were just a collection of blobs
and lines. I do not deny that simple two-dimensional patterns can
sometimes be aesthetically interesting. In Islamic art, where
representation of the human or animal form is forbidden for
theological reasons, the creation of two-dimensional patterns has
reached great heights of sophistication and beauty. Such patterns,
however, often include representations of flowers or specimens
of calligraphy and even the ban on depicting animals and human
beings is not always observed. These facts indicate just how hard
it is for human beings to sustain interest in bare two-dimensional
visual forms.

So, not only is it very difficult psychologically to consider the
formal features of visual art in isolation but most of the time we
should not find it aesthetically interesting to do so.[12] Bell's very
use of the epithet 'significant' in his phrase 'significant form' suggests that he was himself aware that formal patterns alone were of
limited interest. 'Significant', however, does not mean very much
unless we are told what the form which is so described signifies.
When Bell attempts to explain this he falls back on a variant of
expressionism. He offers the suggestion that, 'created form
moves us so profoundly because it expresses the emotion of its
creator'.[13] The artist, according to Bell, sees objects as pure
forms, distinct from any associations they may have or ends that
they may serve, and tries to express the aesthetic emotion which

he feels before such forms by re-creating them in his art. In seeing the significant form of things the artist somehow glimpses 'ultimate reality'. Bell is admittedly very tentative about all this and perhaps it should not be scrutinized too critically. Certainly it will not bear much examination, for the only account Bell offers of the aesthetic emotion which the artist feels before objects and which we in turn feel before successful works of art is a circular one: the aesthetic emotion is what we feel in the presence of significant form. No attempt is made to elaborate the way in which such an emotion is expressed by the artist and the talk of 'ultimate reality' is vague in the extreme. Fry, in *Vision and Design*, speaks of a work which possesses significant form as 'the outcome of an endeavour to express an idea rather than to create a pleasing object' and of the aesthetic emotion being felt to have 'a peculiar quality of "reality" '.[14] This is much the same view as in Bell, expressed more briefly and even more tentatively but no less vaguely.

Of course Bell and Fry were not professional philosophers and they developed their view in order to apply it to the criticism of particular works of art. However, if the claim that the essence and value of visual art lies in significant form is put forward as a general theory, then some defensible account of what 'significant' means here must be produced and this Bell and Fry fail to do.

Bell's concept of significant form was picked up and developed by Susanne Langer in two books, *Philosophy in a New Key*[15] and *Feeling and Form*.[16] Langer directs her attention to the way in which aesthetic forms are significant. She rejects the idea of a specifically aesthetic emotion and argues that the forms of art somehow correspond to formal features of human emotions in general. She talks of forms 'symbolizing' feeling because she thinks they express 'the life of feeling' in an articulate and organized way without having precise meaning of the kind that language has. At bottom Langer's theory is a type of expressionism since she holds that art conveys certain features of human feeling in a special way. She is not altogether successful in explaining just what features are conveyed or just what distinguishes the 'symbolic' way this is done. The attempt to clarify how form conveys feeling leads her into the detailed discussions of the different arts which occupy most of *Feeling and Form*. These discussions concentrate on the formal features of art so that in a way hers too is a formalist theory. It might be described as formalism with an explicitly expressionist basis.

The attempt to make sense of the 'significant' in 'significant form' leads then to a particular kind of expressionism. When we recall that Hanslick also allowed that music could be expressive of certain general features of feelings, although he denied that this was what made it beautiful, we might be tempted to think that so-called formalist theories are merely a subspecies of expressionist theories. Hanslick, Bell, and Fry all take it for granted that art can in some way express emotion and turn their attention to the formal structures by means of which expression is achieved in particular arts. We have seen that Hanslick is suspicious of mixed arts such as opera and a similar suspicion is expressed by Roger Fry.[17] It is true that Susanne Langer in *Feeling and Form* attempts to cover all the arts and refuses to exclude any as mixed or impure. At the same time she stresses the differences between the arts and discusses what others have regarded as 'pure' arts—the visual arts and music—before proceeding to offer accounts of mixed arts in which one art, as she puts it, 'assimilates' another. On the whole formalists are acutely aware of differences between the arts. At first sight this would appear to differentiate them sharply from expressionists such as Croce and Collingwood.[18] It might, however, be another indication that formalists are not really addressing the same questions as Croce and Collingwood addressed. Whereas Croce and Collingwood enquired into the nature of art in general, formalists examine the specific structures in individual arts. Perhaps before formalism can become a general theory of art it must be underpinned by expressionism, as it is in Langer.

Nevertheless, it would be premature at this stage to draw such a conclusion about the nature of formalism and its relationship to expressionism, for we have not yet considered whether the versions of formalism offered by Hanslick, Bell, and Fry *could* be extended to cover all the arts. In particular we have not considered in detail what is meant by formalism in literature. At this point we should recall that the importance of form in literature is often stressed by both literary critics and creative writers. We must now consider not only whether formalist theories of the kind we have been discussing can be extended to cover all the arts but also how closely formalism in literature is related to formalism in the other arts.

Bell and Fry both thought it might be possible to extend their theory of significant form to other arts besides the visual. Bell mentions the possibility of a similar approach to music. He was sceptical about the claims of literature to be 'pure art' in his sense but Fry in *Transformations* considers how the theory might be applied to literature.[19] If we try to develop such an extension in detail we are immediately confronted by the problem that formal features in the different arts seem at first to be of very different kinds. In regarding Hanslick's view of music and Bell's and Fry's view of visual art as parallel we are assuming a parallel between features such as the rhythms and intervals in music and the patterns of shape and colour in visual art. Earlier in this chapter I mentioned the metre used for verse, the ordering of words, and the structure of plot and theme as examples of formal features in literature. There is an obvious parallel between musical rhythm and the metre of verse but we might at first sight suppose that there is not much of a parallel between other formal features of literature and formal features of music or visual art.

However, we saw earlier that when we pick out formal features of a work of art we are in fact concerned with relationships between features. Formalist theories and formalist criticism pay attention not to isolated features but to kinds of relationship. So in the case of music rhythm and intervals, melody and harmony, are not features of individual notes but are constituted by relationships between notes. Hanslick points out the difference between an individual sound and the succession of sounds which is music. Sound is only the material of music and sounds need to be combined and related to one another before we have what can properly be called music.[20] In discussing painting we talk not just about the shapes and colours used but about the balance and the symmetry of the composition, that is, about the relationships between the shapes and colours. Fry in *Vision and Design* describes how his ideal of a spectator looking at Raphael's *Transfiguration* would be someone 'highly endowed with the special sensibility to form who feels the intervals and relations of forms as a musical person feels the intervals and relations of tones', someone 'moved by the pure contemplation of the spatial relations of plastic volumes'.[21]

In the case of literature, verse-metre, word-order, and the structure of plot and theme are all constituted by relationships between other features. Metre is a matter of the relative stresses of words, or the relative length of syllables. The artistic use of word-order exploits the relationship of words to one another both within one sentence and between different sentences.

This may most easily be seen in an example. Let us consider the use of anaphora, the repetition of the opening word or phrase of a clause, in the second paragraph of Dickens's novel, *Bleak House*: 'Fog everywhere. Fog up the river, where it flows among green aits and meadows; fog down the river, where it rolls defiled among the tiers of shipping and the waterside pollutions of a great (and dirty) city. Fog on the Essex marshes, fog on the Kentish heights . . .' The word 'fog' is not only constantly repeated but is emphasized by occurring in the same position in every sentence and clause, that is, by the relationship between the successive occurrences of the word. The anaphora of 'fog' is reinforced by other near-repetitions in deliberately paired phrases: 'up the river', 'down the river'; 'on the Essex marshes', 'on the Kentish heights'. Again this is a matter of the relationships between phrases. The word-order is reinforced by another formal feature, the rhythmic variation in the length of sentences and clauses. We can begin to see how there is, after all, a parallel with the repetition and variation of shapes in a painting or with the repetition, variation, and rhythm of musical phrases. Structure in a work of literature is similarly a matter of relationships between the parts, on a larger scale.

An influential type of formalist literary criticism, namely structuralism, places great stress on the relationships between different elements in a work. Thus David Lodge, in an essay on Thomas Hardy's *Jude the Obscure*, states explicitly that 'we become conscious of form, as readers, through the perception of recurrence and repetition (and the negative kind of repetition which is contrast)' and points out the symmetrical design of the plot of *Jude*: 'As Jude changes from religious belief to scepticism, so Sue changes from scepticism to religious belief. As Arabella changes from worldliness to religiosity and back to worldliness, so Phillotson changes from conventionality to unconventionality and back again to conventionality.' These are symmetrical relationships of a simple and perhaps obvious kind but Lodge goes on to show how, 'Most of the incidents in the novel belong to a series or "set", all the items of which are related to each other either by similarity or by contrast.' He takes as an illustration the recurring incidents of disillusionment or deflation which punctuate Jude's life; a particularly striking example is Jude's first meeting with the vulgarly sensual Arabella just when he is dreaming of academic success at Christminster.[22]

Not only does formalist criticism draw attention to relationships between the elements in a work of art but it will often regard the coherence of those elements into a unified whole as a supreme virtue. Roger Fry, when he attempts to apply the theory of significant form to literature, regards the literary ideal as the creation of a self-contained unified structure and says, 'Comparatively few novelists have ever conceived of the novel as a single perfectly organic esthetic whole.' He also refers to 'the whole organic unity' of a successful tragedy.[23] Similarly, Monroe C. Beardsley, a champion of the American New Criticism, argues that unity is one of three 'general canons' by which works of art should be judged, the others being complexity and intensity.[24] Already in the *Poetics* Aristotle had demanded that a successful tragedy or epic should have a unified plot whose parts cohere to form an ordered whole.[25]

A comprehensive formalist theory which applied to all the arts would be one which saw the essential characteristic of art in its presentation of elements in ordered and unified relationships.[26] Which elements were so presented would vary from one art to another, depending on the medium employed. Here we do seem to have arrived at a general theory which might be set up as a rival to theories of art as imitation and theories of art as expression. Nevertheless, this type of theory differs in an important way from the types of theory considered in the two previous chapters. Unlike them it is concerned solely with the work of art itself. It offers no account of the relationship of the work to its maker or its audience. No claims are made either about the relationship between the work of art and the wider world in which it exists; nothing is said about the work copying that world or in some other way giving us information about it. This concern only with the work of art itself constitutes one of the attractions of formalist theory, for it avoids all the pitfalls which can arise if we consider how the work of art is related to its maker, its audience, and the world at large.

On the other hand, if it is presented simply as a theory which demands coherent ordered relationships among the elements in a work of art, formalism is extremely vague. There are different ways of achieving artistic order and unity and the theory only becomes really meaningful when applied to particular arts and specific examples. A Greek tragedy and a concerto by Bach may both be unified but any analogy between them only becomes interesting if it can be developed in detail. Hanslick, Bell, and Fry were wise to concentrate on the arts they knew best. Formalist criticism is often more impressive than formalist theory because criticism can only benefit from the detailed examination of a work to which formalism leads, whereas formalist theory quickly loses touch with the reality of particular works of art and becomes lost in vague generalizations about 'organic unity' or 'significant form'.

Since formalism is concerned with the relationships between elements in a work of art and since such elements may be of many different kinds, formalist criticism possesses considerable flexibility and may consider many different aspects of a work. We have seen that in the case of literature, the ordering of words and their rhythm, the structure of a plot, and the arrangement of themes could all be considered by a formalist. At the same time a formalist will refuse to consider such matters as the historical context of a work or its relation to its author's life. Moreover, there will be limits to what a strict formalist can say about such matters as imagery or the associations aroused by the words used. Let us return to the passage of *Bleak House* considered earlier. The fog emphasized at the beginning of the book is the metaphorical fog of the law as well as the physical fog over London as the immediately following description of the Court of Chancery makes clear:

Never can there come fog too thick, never can there come mud and mire too deep, to assort with the groping and floundering condition which this High Court of Chancery, most pestilent of hoary sinners, holds this day in the sight of heaven and earth . . . Well may the court be dim, with wasting candles here and there; well may the fog hang heavy in it, as if it would never get out . . .

Attention to the arrangement and rhythm of the words and to the metaphorical use of 'fog' made explicit in the text can help us to appreciate the point Dickens is making. But the reiteration of 'fog' and its metaphorical use here only have point because of what the word 'fog' means literally, because it conjures up specific unpleasant associations for us and would have conjured up even more specific and more unpleasant ones for Dickens's original readers who were living before the days of smokeless zones, in the era of London 'pea-soupers'. Form may be very important in literature but it is not everything.

Formal features are more important in some works than others. A Greek tragedy is more unified and ordered in its plot than a tragedy by Shakespeare. Does that make Sophocles' *Oedipus the King* a better play than Shakespeare's *King Lear*? We might prefer to say that both are fine plays, but that they excel in different ways. Bell and Fry rated Post-Impressionist art, in which form played a particularly important part, more highly than the art which immediately preceded it. Now that the battle they fought has been won and the Post-Impressionists have joined the canon of highly admired artists, their passionate comparisons look dated and strange. Hanslick confined his discussion to purely instrumental music and was inclined to dismiss opera, song, programme music, and pieces with programmatic titles because these types of music are not appreciated for their form alone. While we may recognize that Hanslick offers an acute analysis of the formal features of purely instrumental music, there is no good reason to follow him in valuing less highly music which also excels by other means.

The flexibility of formalist criticism and its concern with the work of art in itself mean that it can offer helpful discussions of a variety of works in the different arts. Yet in the end formalism too, like the theories of art as imitation or expression, cannot cope with the diversity of art. All works of art may be said to have some form and all are a unity in the loose sense in which any individual thing is a unity. Similarly all works of art may be said to exhibit coherence and order in this loose sense. But not all the works of art we regard as successful succeed because of the unified ordering of their elements. A formalist theory expressed in general terms of unity, coherence, and order could be made to fit all works of art without exception only at the price of understanding the terms 'unity', 'coherence', and 'order' so weakly that the theory lost any explanatory power. If generalizations about unity, coherence, and order are to be given content at a theoretical level, formalism needs to be combined with some other type of theory. This is why Susanne Langer combines formalism with expressionism. However, the earlier suggestion that formalist theories are merely a subspecies of expressionist theories was not correct. Formalism can also be combined with imitation-theory, as it is by Aristotle. Works of art are not in the end independent of their makers, their audiences, and the wider world and in the end, however productive it may be as a method of criticism, formalism cannot stand alone as a theory.

The three types of theory considered so far all in the end fail because they cannot do justice to the diversity of examples which art presents. It has begun to look as though there is no satisfactory general theory of what works of art have in common, only criticism of particular works on the one hand and philosophical questions about such matters as imagination and emotion on the other. This suggests that aesthetic theory should concern itself with the nature of our interest in works of art rather than with the nature of the works themselves. Before we pursue this possibility, we should consider a topic mentioned in the introductory chapter but neglected since, namely natural beauty. What qualities make natural beauty an object of aesthetic interest and are these qualities which it shares with works of art? We shall begin the next chapter with this question.

5

Art, beauty, and aesthetic appreciation

Works of art are not the only objects of aesthetic appreciation. People will make trips to visit landscapes they regard as especially beautiful and want to spend time simply looking at the West Highlands of Scotland or the countryside of Provence. Natural beauty may be found in many forms. We can enjoy simply looking at a clump of primroses, a well-groomed horse, or a beautiful woman just as we can enjoy simply looking at mountain scenery. Aesthetic appreciation of nature is not confined to the sense of sight. Our appreciation of a country scene may include listening to the sound of a waterfall or to the song of birds as well as looking at the landscape; we may also take pleasure in the smell of grass after rain or the scent of pine-trees and relish the texture of soft grass, springy heather, or dry autumn leaves as we touch them. Tastes can be appreciated in the same way. Most of the time it is difficult to separate our appreciation of tastes from the satisfaction of hunger and thirst but the true gourmet as he savours his smoked salmon or sips his vintage wine is enjoying the taste for its own sake and it is snobbery to deny that he too is experiencing aesthetic pleasure just as the lover of mountain scenery does.

We should not be misled here by the narrow range of the English word 'beautiful'. In English, landscapes, women, horses, and flowers may be beautiful but men are described as 'handsome' and cows or wine as 'fine' rather than 'beautiful'. Aesthetic appreciation would have a very narrow range of objects if it were confined to those objects to which 'beautiful' happens to be applicable in English. The fact is that English has no term of general aesthetic commendation. Instead there is a related family of terms: 'beautiful', 'pretty', 'lovely', 'fine', 'handsome'. This problem is not peculiar to English. Although the French 'beau' and the German 'schön' both have a wider range than the English 'beautiful', there are contexts in which other terms of aesthetic commendation, such as 'joli' or 'hübsch', are more appropriate.

Both in English and in other languages more specific aesthetic terms, with narrower ranges of application, are also employed, terms such as 'graceful', 'elegant', and 'dainty'.

'Beautiful' and its relatives are used not only of nature and of works of art but also to express aesthetic appreciation of man-made objects not primarily designed as works of art. A girl and her dress may both be called pretty, for instance. It is particularly the more specific aesthetic terms which are readily used of all kinds of man-made objects. Not only women but clothes, mathematical proofs, and computer programmes can be described as elegant. People, movements, and crockery can all be described as dainty.

Aesthetic appreciation may be directed at a variety of natural and man-made objects, perceived by any of the five senses. Yet the theories we have been examining in the last three chapters are all concerned primarily or exclusively with works of art. We must now consider whether any of these theories can be extended so as to offer an account of all objects which afford us aesthetic pleasure.

The theory that art is imitation will not take us very far here, for unless we believe as Plato perhaps did that the natural world is fashioned as an imitation of some divine model[1] there is no way in which natural objects could be thought literally to imitate or represent anything. For an imitation there must be a maker who produces an object intended to represent something else and even if we believe that God has made the natural world there is no need to suppose that he has made it to represent anything else. It would in any case be impossible for us to judge the accuracy of the representation, having no knowledge of the mysterious model. Such speculations bear no relationship to our experience of the beautiful in nature. If asked, 'Why do you admire the hills around Loch Lomond?', we are not going to reply, 'Because they represent the cosmic hills so accurately'.

In discussing representation in Chapter 2 we saw that the nature of artistic representation could best be understood if we considered the role of the imagination in our response to representational art, the way in which we see a haywain in the shapes and colours of Constable's canvas, or enter imaginatively into the situation represented in a play or a novel. This kind of imaginative projection can be applied to natural objects too. We can see shapes in the clouds or hear chattering voices in the sound of a running brook. Such projection, however, plays only a very small part in our aesthetic appreciation of nature. We can enjoy the beauty of the clouds in the evening sky without constructing cloud-capped towers and gorgeous palaces in our imagination. We can listen with pleasure to the running brook without fancying that it represents any other sound. Moreover, we do not suppose that the towers and palaces are really *in* the clouds or the voices really *in* the water, for we know that it is we ourselves who have put them there. We are getting out of nature only what we, as beholders, put into it.

Just as nature has not been designed to represent anything, so it has not been designed to express anything. Aesthetic appreciation of natural beauty can shade into a religious awe before the works of God, for those who believe in him, but there is no reason to regard nature as the expression of the emotions of a divine Artist. Even if nature has been made by God, why should we suppose that he uses it to express human emotions? Intense experience of nature can also come close to a kind of pantheism which sees natural phenomena as pointing beyond themselves, charged with an almost symbolic significance. This is the kind of experience which Wordsworth had and described in such poems as 'Lines composed a few miles above Tintern Abbey' and *The Prelude*. Such exalted experiences fall on the borderline between the aesthetic and the religious. Even in more mundane aesthetic experience we do attribute expressive properties to natural objects: we say that clouds scud restlessly across the sky, that the hills, fields, and olive-trees make up a peaceful scene, that the waves lapping on the shore have a gentle sound.

These properties, however, are not *in* the natural objects, any more than representational properties are. The clouds would not be restless nor the landscape peaceful if there were no one there to look at them. We must study ourselves, not nature, if we want an answer to the question why we find certain natural objects expressive. As with works of art, the answer will be partly a matter of psychology: we may find a landscape peaceful because of the shades of green displayed in it and the question why we find green a restful colour is one for psychology. We shall also have to consider what kind of emotional response is involved. A peaceful landscape may have a directly calming effect on our emotions but it may also affect us less immediately, making us only imagine feeling calm or making us feel calm in a special, detached, 'aesthetic' way.

We saw in Chapters 2 and 3 that in order to understand representation and expression in art it was necessary to turn away from works of art and their properties and consider the nature of our response to them. We began there to explore the roles of imagination and emotion in aesthetic appreciation. This brief consideration of our ascription of representational and expressive properties to natural objects makes it even clearer that an account of aesthetic appreciation is required.

While theories of art as imitation or expression imply an artist who has deliberately designed the work, formalism concentrates on the work of art itself and pays no attention to its maker. It should therefore come as no surprise that formalism applies to natural beauty more easily than other theories do. We can appreciate the arrangement of shapes and colours in a real landscape just as we can appreciate a similiar arrangement in a painted landscape and it makes no difference to such purely formal appreciation that the arrangement of the real landscape has not been designed by an artist. We have seen that formalism is concerned with the relationships between formal features. This means that some complexity of structure is required if we are to appreciate an object's formal qualities. In nature, the most complex objects we appreciate aesthetically are those presented to the sense of sight. Yet examples of aesthetically pleasing formal arrangement are presented to the other senses too. The dawn chorus offers an attractive combination of the songs of different kinds of bird. A patch of moorland may afford a sequence of contrasting textures: soft grass, springy heather, and crisp bracken. With smells and tastes appreciation of formal arrangement becomes less easy since any combination is likely to become a blend.

Appreciation of formal arrangement also plays an important part in our aesthetic response to man-made objects which are not works of art: it is the form of the elegant mathematical proof or computer programme that we pick out for aesthetic approval. A well-planned meal is designed with an eye to balancing different tastes and flavours and our aesthetic appreciation of these, if we can separate it from the satisfaction of hunger, is in part an appreciation of the combination and arrangement of tastes. We should notice that in turning to man-made objects we have turned to objects which even though they are not works of art are deliberately designed to give aesthetic satisfaction. Those who plan the meal are thinking of what will be found pleasing by those who will eat it. The mathematician has in mind the response of those who will consider his proof. It is the consumer or the spectator who will judge whether an arrangement is formally satisfying. The maker attempts to guide their response.

In the case of natural objects, no one else is guiding the way we look, listen, or feel but as beholders we can provide our own guidance. We can choose to look at a landscape from a particular angle or go to a viewpoint from which the shapes of hills are particularly striking. In so doing we are, as it were, 'framing' the landscape. We are looking at it as if it were a painting designed for our inspection. Just as a landscape is not expressive if there is no one there to look at it, so it is not formally satisfying either. Here, too, the nature of our appreciation requires investigation.

We saw in the last chapter that as a general aesthetic theory formalism is extremely vague. This very vagueness facilitates its extension to cover natural beauty. In natural beauty as in works of art many different elements are involved and in appreciating them as form we are appreciating their relationships to one another. But as in art, so in nature it is not only formal relationships that we appreciate. We may admire a golden cornfield, for example, purely for its rich colour, without thinking of the contrast between that colour and the green of the surrounding trees. I said that smells and tastes in nature tend to blend and so are not easily appreciated for their formal arrangement, but this does not mean they are not appreciated aesthetically. It is not form which makes the scent of pine-trees or the smell of a rose aesthetically pleasing. Moreover, some natural phenomena—high, jagged, irregular mountain peaks or rolling peals of thunder—may be appreciated for their very formlessness. I mentioned in the last chapter that Kant gave an account of beauty as form. Kant also distinguished between the beautiful and the sublime and made use of the sublime to account precisely for such natural phenomena as these, which lack regularity and order but are appreciated for that very reason.[2]

None of the theories of art so far considered is entirely satisfactory. None, not even formalism, can be extended so as to cover satisfactorily all aesthetic appreciation of nature and of man-made objects other than works of art. An investigation of aesthetic appreciation itself seems increasingly called for. Before we finally turn in that direction, one other possibility should be considered. Might there be some elusive quality possessed by all the different objects we appreciate aesthetically which explains our interest in them? In a way this would be a much simpler answer than any we have discussed hitherto. Such objects, it might be said, do not all represent something else, they are not all expressive, they are not all appreciated for their formal features, but they all have one crucial quality which elicits aesthetic admiration. English lacks a satisfactory term for this quality but we may call it 'beauty' so long as we remember that it is a quality which may be found in men and wine and even cows as well as in landscapes, women, horses, and flowers, in plays, novels, and concertos as well as in paintings, buildings, and songs. Perhaps instead of spending time on representation, expression, and form we should have been asking one simple question: what is beauty?

I shall consider four types of answer to this question: that beauty is a simple quality not susceptible of further definition; that beauty may be defined in terms of other more specific aesthetic qualities such as grace, elegance, and daintiness; that beauty may be defined in terms of other non-aesthetic qualities; and finally, that the question can only be answered by looking at what sort of judgement we make if we judge something to be beautiful.

First, we might answer the request for a definition of beauty by declaring that it is a simple quality which cannot be further defined in terms of anything else. We recognize it by intuition and there is little more to be said.[3] Such an answer is in effect a refusal to engage in further discussion. It would make disagreements about beauty irresolvable, for if I find the mountains around Loch Lomond beautiful while you are not impressed by them at all, it is simply my intuition of beauty against yours and why should mine be more trustworthy than yours? Comparative aesthetic judgements will also rest on intuition and any attempt to offer reasons for such judgements will become pointless. Why try to explain what makes Alice more beautiful than Barbara if all that is needed is to take a good look at both of them and consult our intuitions? Yet we do engage in discussions about aesthetic matters, we do make aesthetic comparisons, and we do offer reasons for our aesthetic judgements. The claim that beauty is a simple, indefinable quality, recognized by intuition, cannot account for these features of our response to aesthetic objects.

The second type of answer, that beauty may be defined in terms of other more specific aesthetic qualities such as grace, elegance, and daintiness, is attractive to speakers of English. Instead of pressing the word 'beauty' and its adjective 'beautiful' to do a job they do not normally do in our language, why not turn to the whole family of aesthetic terms and say that objects we appreciate aesthetically all possess at least one of the features picked out by this family of terms? The trouble about this family, however, is that it is a very extended one with a good many fringe members. Deciding just which terms to include is even more difficult than deciding which members of an extended family to invite to a wedding reception. In both cases the problem is the same: where shall we draw the line? 'Graceful', 'elegant', and 'dainty' all deserve inclusion, as do 'serene' and 'majestic', but what about 'colourful', 'slender', 'petite', 'glossy'?

Aesthetic terms themselves may be divided into several different groups. Some pick out what are often called 'emergent' qualities of things, qualities such as daintiness or gracefulness which emerge from and depend on other qualities of shape, size, or colour. A very large thing or person cannot be dainty, a small thing or person cannot be majestic, and only things or people which are capable of a certain kind of movement can be graceful. This dependence is itself hard to define. It is not possible to specify a set of necessary and sufficient conditions which must all be satisfied if something is to count as dainty, majestic, or graceful. We have to fall back on saying something like, 'Dainty people are usually small and neat' and on offering examples. Other aesthetic terms, such as 'balanced' or 'well proportioned', pick out formal qualities of objects. Others again, such as 'serene' or 'sombre', pick out expressive qualities. Still others, such as 'charming' or 'amusing', pick out qualities which arouse emotions in us directly.

If we say that beauty is to be defined in terms of more specific aesthetic qualities we are faced with a very large range of qualities of different types. Language is flexible and new words, or new uses of existing words, are constantly being generated so that the range of terms used to pick out specific aesthetic qualities is potentially infinite. These more specific qualities themselves require definition. In particular it remains unclear just how they are related to the qualities which give rise to them, how daintiness, for example, is related to smallness and neatness. Neatness might itself be considered an aesthetic quality: how is it in turn to be defined? In exchanging one term, 'beauty', for a family of terms, we exchange one problem for a family of inter-locking and interrelated problems.[4]

Just as it is unclear how specific aesthetic qualities are related to the aesthetic and non-aesthetic qualities which give rise to them, how daintiness, for example, is related to smallness and neatness, so it is unclear how beauty is related to the non-aesthetic qualities in terms of which we might try to define it. Attempts to define beauty in the third of the ways initially sug-gested run into two kinds of problem. Let us take as an illustra-tion one perennially popular definition which defines beauty as symmetry among the parts of a whole.[5] First, beauty cannot just be identical with symmetry of parts. In calling 'beautiful' an object which is symmetrically proportioned we are doing more than just describing it. There is a gap between the factual descrip-tion, 'symmetrically proportioned', and the aesthetic evaluation, 'beautiful'. This gap is exposed in another way by the second kind of problem. Do we want to say that all and only those objects which have symmetry of parts are beautiful? A mountain range may be lacking in symmetry and yet may be admired aesthetically. Simple colours can be beautiful even though they have no parts to be symmetrically arranged. On the other hand a perfectly regular pattern constantly repeated in a design may be dull, not beautiful. Attempts to define beauty in terms of particu-lar non-aesthetic qualities are always open to counter-examples; suggested definitions are always both too narrow, in failing to include instances of beauty, and too wide, in failing to exclude instances which have the relevant non-aesthetic qualities and yet are not beautiful.

The theories of art as representation, expression, and form may all be seen as attempts to define beauty in terms of non-aesthetic qualities. Indeed, the definition of beauty as symmetry of parts is a version of formalism. We have seen that all these theories fail precisely in not doing justice to the diversity of things which we can appreciate aesthetically in both art and nature. We have seen too that even in the case of works of art which are representational, expressive, or formally ordered, it is not always these qualities which are aesthetically admired and valued. We do not admire representational paintings only for their accuracy in representation; if we did, *trompe-l'œil* paintings would be the most beautiful. In admiring a painting as beautiful, we are doing more than just recognizing its accuracy in representation.

Three of the four ways of defining beauty mentioned on p. 61 have now been considered. All three fail because they cannot account satisfactorily for the nature of aesthetic appreciation and for the relationship between aesthetic judgements and purely descriptive judgements, because they cannot explain how we can offer reasons for our aesthetic judgements, make aesthetic comparisons, and attempt to resolve aesthetic disagreements. The fourth approach, consideration of what sort of judgement we make in judging something to be beautiful, looks the only profitable one. The attempt to discover the nature of beauty thus leads in the same direction as our previous discussions and we must now investigate the nature of aesthetic appreciation and judgement.

Aesthetic appreciation is a complex matter, involving both emotional and intellectual factors. Already in this chapter I have mentioned aesthetic enjoyment, admiration, and approval as well as appreciation, response, and judgement. An account of aesthetic appreciation should give due weight to the emotional element in our response to works of art and natural beauty. This emotional element is often labelled 'aesthetic pleasure' but it can vary from pleasure in its mildest form to rapturous enthusiasm. We should not forget that there are also negative aesthetic responses. Works of art and other aesthetic objects can be ugly instead of beautiful and can arouse the reverse of pleasure in varying degrees from mild distaste to utter disgust. Aesthetic pleasure is manifested in a desire to continue or repeat the experience. We want to stop at the viewpoint and look at the scenery, we want to revisit beautiful places or reread books we have enjoyed. Correspondingly the reverse of aesthetic pleasure is manifested in a desire to get away from the offending object. Not only do we want to continue or repeat a pleasurable aesthetic experience but we regard doing so as an end in itself. We say that we are looking at the scenery or reading the book just because it gives us pleasure to do so. The gourmet who has aesthetic experiences of taste enjoys the taste of smoked salmon for its own sake, not to satisfy his hunger.

Aesthetic pleasure and its reverse must be distinguished from the other emotions which expressive works of art and natural objects may arouse in us, emotions as varied as sadness, anger, love, or amusement. A tragedy may arouse pity and fear in the spectators and yet they take pleasure in watching it. It is these other emotions which are often said to be aroused in a special, detached, 'aesthetic' way.

A satisfactory account of aesthetic appreciation must explain both aesthetic pleasure and aesthetic detachment. At the same time it must find room for the intellectual element in aesthetic response. When we judge something to be beautiful or approve its aesthetic qualities, intellectual evaluation is involved. If it were not, we could never give reasons for our aesthetic judgements, and aesthetic disagreements would always be irresolvable.

The fundamental account of aesthetic appreciation was offered by Kant in his *Critique of Aesthetic Judgement*. Although the concentration on aesthetic judgement might suggest a purely intellectual approach, Kant's account does make some room for the emotional elements in aesthetic response. Kant uses the term 'aesthetic judgement' in a broad sense which includes both what he calls 'the judgement of taste' and the judgement of the agreeable or the pleasant. By the judgement of taste Kant means the aesthetic judgement in the narrow sense in which we have been using the term. For Kant the prime example of the judgement of taste is 'This is beautiful'.

Kant begins his discussion by distinguishing aesthetic judgements in his broad sense from cognitive or logical judgements which give us knowledge. Whereas in a cognitive judgement such as 'This is red' we are applying a concept 'red' to the object we perceive before us, an aesthetic judgement does not apply any concept to the object but tells us how the person who makes the judgement is reacting to the object. Kant then goes on to distinguish within the sphere of aesthetic judgement between the judgement of taste and the judgement of the agreeable. The judgement of the agreeable concerns something which simply gratifies the senses, for example pleasant-tasting food which we desire to consume. Judgements of taste on the other hand are disinterested. By this Kant does not mean that they are unbiased or impartial, nor does he mean that we find their objects boring. He means that such judgements are not determined by any needs or wants of ours concerning the object. We have, as he puts it, no interest in 'the real existence of the object'; we have no desire to make use of it for a further end but wish only to contemplate it as it appears to us.

Yet Kant does not think that in judging an object to be beautiful we are doing no more than expressing our subjective reaction, for he points out that judgements of taste claim universal validity. In other words, when we say, 'This is beautiful' we are claiming that others should agree with our judgement, a claim we would not be making if all we said was, 'I like this'. We cannot be claiming that others should apply to the object the same concept as we do, since on Kant's view we are not here applying a concept at all. What we are claiming is that others should have the same reaction to the object as we do.

The claim of universal validity concerns the subject who makes the judgement, not the object judged. Kant is not saying that there are rules which determine when it is proper to call an object beautiful. On the contrary he holds that judgements of taste are singular, that is, they judge only one particular object and they judge that object in itself, not as an example of its kind. Suppose that in a garden I come upon a glossy red tulip, just out, with its petals fitting together in smooth curves. If I judge the tulip to be beautiful I am implying that others should agree with me but I am making no claims about tulips in general. I am not applying any rule which says that all glossy red tulips with smoothly curved petals are beautiful. The basis of my judgement is how this particular tulip strikes me at this moment.

Kant also introduces a distinction between free and dependent beauty. In a judgement of taste properly so called we judge an object as an example of free beauty. If we consider an object as a good example of its kind, that is an impure judgement of taste, in which the object is judged as an example of dependent beauty. So we might admire a fine Persian cat considered by itself as an example of free beauty but if we compare the cat with others and give it first prize in a pedigree cat show we are treating it as an example of dependent beauty.

Kant picks out the peculiar character of judgements of taste in a negative way, by contrasting aesthetic judgements in general with logical ones and then contrasting judgements of taste in particular with judgements where we have an interest in the object's existence. Similarly, the account he offers of our reaction to objects we judge aesthetically contrasts implicitly with his account of how we come to know things. On Kant's theory of knowledge perception presents us with a chaotic mass of sensations. These are organized by the imagination and the understanding which bring them together under concepts. This is what happens when I see the tulip as a tulip and as red. When I see the tulip as beautiful, however, the imagination and the understanding are in 'free play', I am contemplating the tulip without bringing it under a concept. Exactly what is meant by 'the free play of imagination and understanding' is not very clear. Kant is trying to describe some kind of mental activity which is not knowing and yet involves the capacity to make judgements, albeit judgements of a peculiar kind. According to Kant we take pleasure in this 'free play of imagination and understanding'; this, for him, is aesthetic pleasure. Since everyone must have the same cognitive faculties of imagination and understanding if knowledge is to be communicable at all, everyone is capable of this 'free play' and so of feeling aesthetic pleasure.

Kant thinks that when we judge an object to be an example of free beauty we are judging its form alone because we are not applying a concept to it and have no interest in its existence. Forms that we find aesthetically satisfying seem to have a kind of purposiveness or finality, that is, they are organized as if there were some purpose they fulfilled. The smooth curves of the tulip seem to be fitted together by design. But this is 'purposiveness without purpose' or 'finality without end'.[6] There is no obvious end or purpose served by the smooth fit of the curved petals. Even if there did turn out to be some purpose, we would not be concerned with it when we judge the tulip aesthetically, for in such a judgement we are concentrating on the appearance of the tulip and on nothing else. In the case of dependent beauty, however, we do apply a concept to the object and in so doing treat the object as fulfilling a further end. If we give the fine Persian cat first prize in the cat show, we are judging it with the perfection of Persian cats as a species in mind. Such perfection is an end in the sense that it determines what a Persian cat ought to be like. If we are thinking of how the cat before us measures up to this ideal we are not judging the cat in purely aesthetic terms.

Kant's account of beauty as form places excessively severe restrictions on what can count as the object of aesthetic appreciation. His distinction between 'free' and 'dependent' beauty and his discussion of the sublime may be seen as attempts to mitigate this. His talk of 'the free play of imagination and understanding' is puzzlingly obscure even when it is related to his theory of knowledge.[7] Nevertheless, his account of the logical character of aesthetic judgement successfully picks out its distinguishing features. These require further examination. I propose now to consider in turn the disinterestedness of aesthetic judgements, their claim to universal validity, and their singular nature.

The notion that aesthetic judgements are disinterested was common in the eighteenth century[8] but it is Kant's use of the idea which has been influential on subsequent aesthetic theory. The idea was given great importance by Schopenhauer who thought that in aesthetic experience we contemplate objects in a pure and detached way free from the demands of the will and from the constraints of our individual personality. Unlike Kant, Schopenhauer thought that such contemplation did give us knowledge of a special kind, knowledge of what Schopenhauer called the Platonic Ideas, the universal perceived in the particular.[9]

Schopenhauer's view is expressed in terms of his metaphysical system. Edward Bullough's theory of 'psychical distance' offers a similar view founded on a psychological rather than a metaphysical basis. Bullough claimed that in order to appreciate objects aesthetically we must distance ourselves from all practical concerns with them. He illustrated this idea with the example of experiencing a fog at sea. The fog has a strange effect on the sound and appearance of everything which can only be appreciated if we distance ourselves from fears about the ship coming to grief or from the sailor's practical concern with how best to navigate in these circumstances. Bullough then proceeded to apply the theory in more detail to works of art and especially to drama. Some degree of distance is necessary if we are to experience a play properly. Aesthetic appreciation will fail if we are too much involved personally in the events on stage: the person in the grip of jealousy is not the one best able to appreciate *Othello*. On the other hand, if we distance ourselves too far, the objects will simply leave us cold, as happens in melodrama where we do not feel involved with the characters at all.[10]

It is still a very common idea that one of the distinguishing marks of the aesthetic attitude is detachment, distance, or disinterestedness, that in contemplating something aesthetically we are removed from all practical concerns with the object. Such an idea does capture a familiar feature of aesthetic experience and yet it is not easy to give a positive account of the aesthetic attitude in these terms. Whether we speak of detachment, distance, or disinterestedness we are always offering a negative definition, pointing out what the aesthetic attitude is *not*—it is not moral, economic, practical, etc. If we ask, 'What then *is* it if it is not all these things?' the only positive account offered by most writers is a psychological one. Kant talks in mysterious terms of 'the free play of imagination and understanding'; Schopenhauer imposes his own metaphysical interpretation upon the psychological experience and describes the aesthetic attitude in terms of the intellect freeing itself from the demands of the will; Bullough, assuming that we all know introspectively what distancing ourselves is like, presents us with suggestive examples rather than any extended analysis.

A highly complex and sophisticated psychological account has been offered by the Polish thinker Roman Ingarden who as a phenomenologist tries to describe the contents of experience as accurately as possible.[11] Ingarden claims to detect a series of phases in the aesthetic experience. The object is progressively distanced from practical concerns and we experience not one emotional response but three, at three different stages in the distancing process. Ingarden admits that not all aesthetic experiences go through all the phases he picks out but he offers little in the way of argument to convince the sceptic that even some aesthetic experience is like this. Such introspective psychological accounts are always vulnerable to the claim that our own experience is not like that. If I say that I have never had the experience Ingarden describes and do not know what it is like, who can contradict me?

In order to develop a more defensible account of the aesthetic attitude we need to consider more closely what makes us speak of detachment or disinterestedness here. The reason is the peculiar way in which our emotions are aroused in aesthetic appreciation. The attempt to give some account of this leads to the unsatisfactory psychological element in descriptions of the aesthetic attitude. At the end of Chapter 3 I suggested that feeling an emotion in the detached way appropriate to art might be one particular way of imagining an emotion. We can now take this suggestion a little further. It should be noted that such imagining is possible before any object we contemplate aesthetically, before expressive natural objects as well as before works of art. Let us use a contrast to bring out more clearly the particular kind of imagining an emotion which is in question here. When we daydream, when we conjure up scenes and people in our own minds and imagine our reactions to them, we imagine feeling emotions but this is different from the imagining involved in aesthetic experience. Daydreaming is free to wander at will as the response to a work of art is not. As we saw in Chapter 3, in literature and representational painting what is represented will limit the range of appropriate emotional reactions. In music, a title such as 'Funeral March' may guide our response and even where there is no such title, formal features of the work place some restrictions on the kind of emotion appropriate. There might be disagreement about whether we should describe Mozart's Clarinet Concerto as 'cheerful', as I did in Chapter 3, or as 'serenely happy', but it is clear that it could not sensibly be described as 'mournful', nor as 'anguished'. Our emotional reactions to a work of art are to some extent controlled by the work even if not entirely determined by it.

Much the same is true of expressive properties in nature although here the degree of control is less because we as beholders have more freedom to select what we direct our attention towards. Suppose two people looking at a landscape of farms, some cultivated land, and rolling hills. One might find it peaceful, while the other declared that it presented a scene of busy activity. For the first spectator the scene would conjure up feelings of peace and calm while the second would envisage emotions which accompany brisk efficiency and energetic action. It is unlikely that both these spectators would be concentrating on the same features of the landscape. The first might be looking at the shapes of the hills and the soft shades of green while the second had his eye caught by the farm workers going about their business. Different aspects of the landscape would be arousing different emotions in them. Something like this may happen with works of art too—it could happen, for instance, with a painting of such a scene—but it is less common just because the artist by choosing which features to bring into prominence can more closely control how we see or hear the work and how we react.

Feeling an emotion in the detached way appropriate to aesthetic contemplation is then a particular kind of imagining an emotion. The difference from other kinds of imagining is that our imagined emotions are to some extent controlled by the object contemplated. Our imagination is given some freedom but not total freedom. The detachment arises because we know the emotions are not 'for real'. They do not move us to action. This can be seen more clearly if we consider the way we behave before objects we regard aesthetically. We look at them, listen to them, taste, smell, touch, or feel them, as appropriate, but what is striking is what we do *not* do. We do not take action to rescue the character in the play who is about to be killed, we do not try to shake hands with statues or walk into pictures. The person who contemplates the fog at sea aesthetically will probably infuriate the sailors who are trying to steer the ship since he just stands there admiring it and doing nothing. Although it is easier to characterize 'aesthetic behaviour' negatively in this way, it is also possible to characterize it positively in terms of paying close attention to objects for their own sake.[12] If asked to explain our interest in such objects we will simply draw attention to features of them. Thus if asked, 'Why are you looking at that tulip?' I will say something like, 'Because of its lovely colour and its well-shaped petals'. I am also likely to spend longer than normal looking at the tulip and I might go back for another look later on. I said earlier that a desire to continue or repeat the experience was a manifestation of aesthetic pleasure and another kind of answer I might offer to 'Why are you looking at that tulip?' is 'Because it gives me pleasure to do so'. We do for their own sake things that give us pleasure. In itself this would not serve to pick out aesthetic pleasure from other kinds. I can enjoy playing tennis for its own sake, not in order to win, but that does not mean playing tennis is an aesthetic activity. This is another way of saying that disinterested behaviour is not in itself enough to pick out aesthetic activity. All aesthetic activity is disinterested but not all disinterested activity is aesthetic.

The aesthetic attitude is characterized both by a particular kind of behaviour—attending to objects for their own sake—and by a distinctive kind of emotional response—imagining the emotions appropriate to the object contemplated. But there is more to aesthetic appreciation than taking up an aesthetic attitude towards things. When we go to see a play, for example, we do more than pay attention and respond in the appropriate way. We also want to share our reactions. We want to discuss the play with other people and make judgements upon it. Too much concentration on the aesthetic attitude can obscure the intellectual elements in aesthetic appreciation. We must now return to these and consider the claim of aesthetic judgements to universal validity.

Kant saw the claim to universal validity as one of the crucial differences between the judgement of taste and the judgement of the agreeable. (The other difference, he thought, was the disinterested nature of the judgement of taste.) In this he was surely right. There is more to aesthetic appreciation than the expression of individual preferences. If there were not, aesthetic disputes would be not only irresolvable but pointless. There would be no more sense in trying to persuade someone who finds the plays of Samuel Beckett boring that *Waiting for Godot* is a good play than in trying to persuade someone who does not like custard that they could enjoy it if only they understood it better.

Whereas in judgements which apply a concept, such as 'This is red', there are agreed standards of evidence, in the judgement of taste there are no such standards, since, in Kant's view, we are claiming that others should have the same reaction to the object. We cannot be sure that everyone will, in fact, agree with us but we express our judgement in a way which claims that they ought to do so. This too is, I think, correct. An aesthetic dispute is about reactions to a natural object or a work of art, not about objective characteristics of the thing. Suppose that you do not find the red tulip that has just opened out in the garden as beautiful as I do. If I try and persuade you to share my view I may well draw attention to features of the tulip—the glossiness of the petals, the smoothness of the curves, and so on—but I will be doing so in order to get you to exclaim, 'Ah yes! *Now* I see that it's beautiful.' What I want is for you to react as I do and I shall not be satisfied if you say, 'Yes, very beautiful' and turn away in boredom. Similarly, I shall not be satisfied if you read books about Beckett, agree in a neutral tone that *Waiting for Godot* is after all a good play, and yet still shuffle your feet in boredom when I take you to see it. We need not accept Kant's account of the reaction to beauty as the free play of imagination and understanding in order to accept his view that in judging something to be beautiful we are claiming that others should share our reaction rather than laying down what the thing is like.

The singular nature of the judgement of taste is also relevant here. There are no rules for what counts as beauty in tulips which I can learn and apply and pass on to others. What matters is the experience of this particular tulip. You cannot come to share my view unless you come into the garden and look at the tulip for yourself. You cannot tell whether this one will be beautiful just by thinking about other tulips you have seen in the past. Kant sets this point out clearly in section 33 of the *Critique of Aesthetic Judgement* which begins, 'Proofs are of no avail whatever for determining the judgement of taste'.

The importance of personal experience in aesthetics can also be seen, from a different angle, if we consider that aesthetically striking objects are often felt to force themselves upon our attention. The beautiful tulip stands out from the others, it catches my eye and makes me stop and look at it.[13] Yet not all aesthetic experience is like this. Particularly with complex objects such as works of art we may need to learn a good deal about the object and how to look at it. *Waiting for Godot* may seem boring if we come to it accustomed to the more numerous characters and more eventful plots of traditional drama. We need to understand Beckett's subversion of traditional dramatic conventions, to learn to attend to his use of language and his exploitation of a very undramatic situation. All this in itself will not make the play attractive to us. What it can do is help us towards a personal response to it. Then one day, to put it colloquially, the play grabs us. Perhaps only an individual passage, perhaps a whole scene suddenly strikes home and at last we can begin to appreciate the play properly. Being 'grabbed' by the play is only the beginning of aesthetic appreciation, not the whole story, but until we are 'grabbed' we are not having an aesthetic experience at all. Up to that point we are just accumulating bits of knowledge.

If personal experience is so important, what use is the claim that aesthetic judgements have universal validity? To Kant this view is a claim that others should react as we do to a given object. Yet if judgements of taste are singular and concern only one object taken by itself, it is hard to see how we can argue for such judgements. How can I change your reactions to a tulip or to a play if I cannot appeal to any evidence about tulips or plays in general? Aesthetic disputes may not be pointless but without 'proofs to determine the judgement' how can such disputes be settled? Kant says a little about how aesthetic disputes arise and implies how they might be resolved but he says hardly anything about how one might justify an aesthetic judgement or how comparative aesthetic judgements are possible.

Kant implies that aesthetic disputes can arise in either of two ways. First, it might be the case that the disputing parties are not in fact both making judgements of taste. One of them might be mistaken about his own reactions and think that he was judging something to be beautiful when in fact he was only expressing a personal preference. Presumably in this case he would think his imagination and understanding were in free play when they were not. This idea is hard to make sense of in psychological terms although it might be that in such a case the behaviour of the person making the mistake would display his error. He might, for example, call a peach beautiful but then proceed to pick it up and eat it, thus showing that his judgement of it was not a disinterested judgement of taste but only a judgement of the agreeable.

The second way in which, for Kant, aesthetic disputes can arise is more significant. At the end of section 16 Kant envisages a case in which two people are in dispute because one of them is judging an object as an example of free beauty, that is, with a judgement of taste properly so called, while the other is judging it as an example of dependent beauty, that is, considering how far it is a perfect example of its kind. So I might judge my red tulip to be beautiful while you might think that it is not tall enough to be a perfect specimen of a tulip and so is not beautiful. The difference between us is that we are regarding different features of the tulip as relevant to our assessment of its beauty. To get you to agree that the tulip is beautiful I have to persuade you to look at it without thinking about its lack of height, concentrating instead on the features of colour and shape which give rise to *my* experience and *my* judgement.[14]

These hints in Kant do not give us much clue as to what features are relevant to an aesthetic assessment or how they can provide some kind of justification despite the absence of 'proofs'. Kant's talk of purposiveness without purpose is rather vague and in any case relates to the judgement of an object's form. Not only form is beautiful and not all judgements of taste are judgements of beauty, as Kant himself partly recognizes. Furthermore a Kantian judgement of taste seems not to admit of degrees. Might not two tulips both be freely beautiful but one be more beautiful than the other? In judging more complex objects and works of art we are even more likely to make aesthetic comparisons.[15]

The questions which Kant's view of aesthetic judgement leaves unanswered are important ones. The problems of how aesthetic disputes may be resolved, how aesthetic judgements may be justified, and how aesthetic comparisons are possible all become particularly acute in relation to works of art. Volumes are written offering criticism of works of art; there are professional critics who earn their living by offering assessments of works; there are teachers who profess to educate people in the appreciation of literature, music, painting, and the other arts. If there are no agreed criteria in aesthetics and what matters is personal experience of individual works, are all these people wasting their time? It is all very well to say that aesthetic judgements claim universal validity, but how can this claim be substantiated? This is the problem which we must confront in the next chapter.

6

Criticism, interpretation, and evaluation

We have seen that Kant held both that aesthetic judgements claim universal validity and that there are no proofs which determine such judgements. I argued that he was fundamentally correct on both these points. What is lacking in Kant is any developed account of how the claim of aesthetic judgements to universal validity can be substantiated. I mentioned three problems in particular which Kant leaves unsolved: how aesthetic disputes may be resolved, how aesthetic judgements may be justified, and how aesthetic comparisons are possible. If we had a satisfactory account of the justification of aesthetic judgements, that would explain how aesthetic disputes may be resolved since such disputes typically occur between people who offer differing aesthetic judgements of the same object. Aesthetic comparisons are a particular kind of aesthetic judgement and if we understood how 'Alice is beautiful' may be justified, we could also understand how 'Alice is more beautiful than Barbara' may be justified. The central question of the three thus concerns the justification of aesthetic judgements and my discussion will concentrate on this topic. I shall give some consideration to aesthetic disputes since examination of them helps to clarify how aesthetic judgements are justified.

I said that all three Kantian problems become particularly acute in relation to works of art. Accordingly I propose to discuss the justification of aesthetic judgements by considering the criticism of works of art. Aesthetic judgements of objects in the natural world do not rest upon so sophisticated and complex an edifice of criticism. Essentially, though, judgements in both spheres are supported in the same kind of way and we shall see at the end of the chapter that the critical appreciation of works of art bears a strong resemblance to the aesthetic appreciation of nature. There are, however, further questions which arise in relation to the arts alone and which will be considered in subsequent chapters. Although much of what I have to say will be applicable to criticism of all the arts, since this book is particularly concerned with aesthetics in relation to literature I shall concentrate on literature from now on.

In this chapter I shall consider what kind of justification can be offered for the critical interpretation and evaluation of a work of art. We shall see that the nature of critical arguments suggests that there is no one correct interpretation and evaluation of a given work. In the next chapter I shall consider ways in which the range of possible interpretations and evaluations of a work might be limited and in particular the suggestion that an interpretation is incorrect if it takes no account of the artist's intention. Those who interpret works of literature often talk in terms of their meanings. In Chapter 8 I shall discuss whether, and in what sense, works of literature have meaning and whether, if works do have meaning, they can also state truth. The questions concerning intention and meaning, to be discussed in Chapters 7 and 8, relate primarily to interpretation rather than evaluation. In the final chapter I shall return to evaluation and shall examine whether works of art can or should be evaluated purely in aesthetic terms. In particular I shall consider whether moral considerations are relevant to the evaluation of art. Before we proceed to the detailed questions to be discussed in Chapters 7, 8, and 9, we need some overall picture of how criticism proceeds, of how critics argue both when interpreting and when evaluating works. This chapter will sketch such a picture.

We may begin by looking more closely at Kant's statement that 'Proofs are of no avail whatever for determining the judgement of taste'.[1] There is an implied contrast here between the kind of argument, whatever it might be, that leads to a judgement of taste and a logical argument which proceeds from premises to conclusion by means of deductive reasoning. Suppose I am trying to convince you that *Waiting for Godot* is a good play. I may appeal to Beckett's use of language, to his exploitation of a situation, to his original treatment of dramatic conventions. Yet none of these points compel the conclusion that *Waiting for Godot* is a good play. You may accept everything I say and still fail to agree that the play deserves my favourable evaluation.

In such a situation you are likely to object that *Waiting for Godot* fails to meet certain criteria you would expect a good play to meet. You might, for example, object not just that nothing much happens in the play but that in a way it has no shape, no beginning, middle, or end. The situation depicted in the play has been in existence before the play began, and will continue after it stops. This is made clear by some of what the characters say, by the fact that the two acts take place in the same spot on successive days, and by the repetition in the second act of some of the action of the first act. In particular, in both acts a boy arrives towards the end to tell the two waiting tramps, Vladimir and Estragon, that Godot will not come this evening but will come tomorrow. The structure, or rather the lack of structure, of *Waiting for Godot* partially violates the well-established principle, derived from Aristotle, that a drama should have a beginning, a middle, and an end.[2] To overcome your objection I shall have to argue that in this particular play that criterion is not important. The features which make *Waiting for Godot* a good play are not the same as the features which make *Oedipus the King* a good play and the features which make *Oedipus the King* a good play are not the same as the features which make *King Lear* a good play. All we can say is that there are features often or usually found in good plays. A clear structure of beginning, middle, and end is one such feature and the occurrence of action in the play is another, related feature. But there are good plays, such as *Waiting for Godot*, which do not have these features and there are plays, such as Shakespeare's *Titus Andronicus*, which have a clear structure and plenty of action but fail to be good. There are no necessary and sufficient conditions for a play being good. Moreover, whether a play does have a feature such as a clear structure may itself be a matter of debate. Terms like 'clear structure' are not rigidly defined and already carry some evaluative implications. If we think that *Titus Andronicus* is not a good play, and we expect good plays to have a clear structure, we shall be tempted to argue that despite a superficial appearance of structure the play is not *really* well structured.[3]

So far I have been arguing only that there are no necessary and sufficient conditions for what makes a good play, no universally agreed criteria. Still less are there criteria which we can apply across the genres of literature. What makes *Waiting for Godot* a good play may be different from what makes *Middlemarch* a good novel or *The Waste Land* a good poem. Failure to appreciate unfamiliar literature often arises from our natural tendency to extrapolate from the works we know to the unfamiliar works, to judge the unfamiliar by criteria derived from the familiar. We may fail to appreciate *Waiting for Godot* because we expect it to conform to standards derived from traditional drama. Similarly, we may fail to appreciate *The Waste Land* because we expect it to conform to standards derived from Romantic poetry. To come to appreciate these works, to come to see why they are aesthetically valuable, we must learn to judge them by appropriate criteria. Yet if there are no agreed criteria for aesthetic evaluation it is hard to see how that can be done, how we can know which criteria are appropriate and which are not.

We have met again the same problem which we met in Chapter 5, that aesthetic qualities cannot be defined in terms of non-aesthetic qualities. We saw there that the problem was not solved by substituting more specific aesthetic qualities such as grace, elegance, and daintiness for the general aesthetic quality of beauty. So here it does not help to say that a good play is often or usually one which has a clear structure, for even if that is true we shall have the same kind of problem in defining what constitutes a clear structure.

To demand that critics argue from agreed premisses to a conclusion, in accordance with the method of deductive logic, would lead only to a barren positing of literary rules which would immediately be broken by any artist of originality. Time and again in the history of literature when the characteristics of a particular genre have been rigidly codified great works have then been written which paid no heed to such rules. In the Renaissance Aristotle's statement in the *Poetics* that tragedy attempts as far as possible to keep to one revolution of the sun, or not much more or less, was transformed into the inflexible demand that the time covered by the action of a play should be the same as the time occupied by a performance.[4] Most of the plays of Shakespeare, including some of the greatest, fail to conform to any such rule. The same applies to the other arts. The 'laws' of perspective are conventions which an artist may exploit, not a code by which paintings must be judged. If Beethoven had conformed to established 'rules' of composition, he would not have begun his First Symphony with a discord. Instead of demanding that critical judgements should be justified by universally agreed criteria we should look for a different model which will give us a better understanding of how critical argument proceeds. Before we can develop such a model we need to distinguish three different kinds of critical activity: description, interpretation, and evaluation.

Consider again my imaginary discussion of *Waiting for Godot* and in particular the way in which I suggested that my opponent might argue that *Waiting for Godot* was not a good play. Some of what I attributed to my imaginary opponent described features of the play. For example, I said that in both acts a boy arrives towards the end to tell the two tramps that Godot will not come this evening but will come tomorrow. Some of what I attributed to my opponent was interpretation. We are not told explicitly that the situation depicted was in existence before the play began and will continue after it stops. That is an interpretation, based on the features that have been described. A critical discussion of a work of literature is in practice extremely unlikely to limit itself to description—we should not take much interest in it if it did—and the description will be governed by the interpretation being put forward. Those features will be selected for description which support the interpretation that is being advanced. So in my brief remarks about *Waiting for Godot* I picked on the repeated scene with the boy as the feature of the play which most clearly supports the interpretative point that the situation depicted was in existence before the play began and will continue after it stops. Interpretation itself takes place on more than one level. I was interpreting *Waiting for Godot* when I said that the situation depicted has been in existence before the play began and will continue after it stops. I was still interpreting when I attributed to my imaginary opponent the view that the play lacks shape and has no beginning, middle, or end. The first, lower-level interpretative statement supported the second, more general interpretative statement in the same way as the description of the repeated scene with the boy supported the initial interpretative statement. Since there is such a close link between description and interpretation and since descriptive statements are used to support interpretative statements in the same way as specific, lower-level interpretative statements are used to support more general, higher-level interpretative statements, some theorists would deny that there is any worthwhile distinction to be made between description and interpretation. It is, however, worth making the distinction in theory while recognizing that in practice the two are closely linked and may even shade into one another.[5]

In the imaginary discussion of *Waiting for Godot* I say that despite its lack of shape the play is a good one. Here I am evaluating the play and I am denying that the interpretation given leads to a certain evaluation, namely that the play is bad. My whole argument that there are no necessary and sufficient conditions for what makes a good play appears to suggest that we can make a firm distinction between interpretation and evaluation. If there is a gap in the critic's argument, a point at which one statement ceases to support another, then we seem to have found it. Some theorists would indeed see a yawning gap here and would argue that critics should concern themselves with interpretation only, leaving evaluation to the realms of subjective preference. One of the best known advocates of this position is Northrop Frye in *The Anatomy of Criticism*. In that book Frye develops a system of literary classification, intended to give criticism a scientific structure and so to assist in the interpretation of works of literature. He argues for a sharp split between criticism and 'the history of taste' and declares:

The demonstrable value-judgement is the donkey's carrot of literary criticism and every new critical fashion . . . has been accompanied by a belief that criticism has finally devised a definitive technique for separating the excellent from the less excellent. But this always turns out to be an illusion of the history of taste. Value-judgements are founded on the study of literature; the study of literature can never be founded on value-judgements. Shakespeare, we say, was one of a group of English dramatists working around 1600, and also one of the great poets of the world. The first part of this is a statement of fact, the second a value-judgement so generally accepted as to pass for a statement of fact. But it is not a statement of fact. It remains a value-judgement and not a shred of systematic criticism can ever be attached to it.[6]

However, interpretation and evaluation are not as easily separated as Frye believes. This can be seen in two ways. First, when we look more closely at the practice of literary criticism it becomes clear that some interpretative statements already carry implicit evaluations. Consider the following passage from a discussion of Shakespeare's *The Tempest* by Derek Traversi. Traversi has been going through the play arguing for his interpretation of it as a drama of judgement and reconciliation. When he comes to the masque which Prospero sets before Ferdinand and Miranda at the beginning of Act IV he has this to say:

The rather perfunctory masque, commonplace in spite of its involved stressing of the images of fertility and love, is scarcely necessary after the brief scenes which it is intended to ratify. The best of it, and the most germane to the general purpose, is the song shared between them by the spirits representing Juno and Ceres, where the note of fruitfulness is most directly and least artificially expressed, and where the season of birth and that of autumnal fulfilment are bound together in a manner that reminds us of a similar union in *The Winter's Tale*:

> Spring come to you at the farthest
> In the very end of harvest.

As a whole, however, and in spite of lines which contribute to the central conception, it is hard to deny that this interlude, like its not altogether dissimilar predecessor in *Cymbeline*, belongs more to the structural unity of the play than to its intimate poetic sensibility.[7]

Here Traversi offers an interpretation of the masque's relevance to the rest of the play. He selects as significant the song which expresses 'the note of fruitfulness' and he points out how the song binds together spring, 'the season of birth', and autum, the season of harvest and fulfilment. Because this song is the part of the masque which relates most closely to the general purpose of the play as Traversi understands it, he calls it 'the best' of the masque. Otherwise his unfavourable evaluation of the scene is evident in his description of the masque as 'perfunctory' and 'commonplace'. When he says at the end of the passage quoted, 'this interlude . . . belongs more to the structural unity of the play than to its intimate poetic sensibility' this apparently interpretative remark, in the context, carries clear evaluative implications.

Styles of criticism vary a good deal. Some critics concentrate more on interpretation, others more on evaluation. Most of Traversi's discussion of *The Tempest* is interpretative rather than evaluative. Yet we must recognize that by implication he is arguing all the time for a favourable evaluation of the play as a whole. It is because he does not rate the masque scene as highly as the rest that he has to make explicit his view that it is 'perfunctory' and 'commonplace'. If he failed to do this, the masque might appear to be included in his generally favourable judgement of the play. An evaluation can only be argued for by means of a detailed interpretation and description of the work. The critic must pick out those features of the work which support his evaluation. Indeed, a favourable evaluation is usually implied in the very choice of a work as a subject for interpretation. Here we come to the second way in which evaluation and interpretation are connected.

Critics do not devote the attention to interpreting the novels of Barbara Cartland that they devote to those of Jane Austen. It might be thought that this is due to prejudice, that critics tend to concern themselves with works of literature popularly regarded as 'highbrow' and that there is no reason why a literary critic could not profitably discuss the work of Barbara Cartland. However, there is more involved here than conventional prejudice. It is not true that critics simply accept the canon of works of literature accepted in their society. Critics often play a significant role in altering the canon, for example by bringing back into favour works which have been neglected. Thus the critical efforts of T.S.Eliot and others in this century have brought about a renewed interest in the seventeenth-century English metaphysical poets. If a critic wants to show us that a work is aesthetically valuable and deserves our attention, he or she must show us that there is matter there to be interpreted, that the work repays critical study. The reason why the novels of Barbara Cartland are less studied by critics than the novels of Jane Austen is that they are less rewarding to study. Interpretation of them will be exhausted much sooner than interpretation of Jane Austen's novels. No doubt Barbara Cartland's novels could profitably be studied from another point of view. We could study what makes them so popular and successful and discover the sociological and psychological reasons why they appeal to a wide public but that would be a different kind of enquiry. It would not be literary criticism. In general a work which is rich in possibilities of interpretation will be a work which we find aesthetically valuable and conversely a work poor in interpretative possibilities will lack aesthetic value.

A similar structure of description, interpretation, and evaluation is used in criticism of the other arts too. All three are combined in this sentence from Michael Levey on Botticelli's *The Birth of Venus* (see Plate 3): 'Perfect harmony reigns throughout the composition, symbolized in the weightless pose and poise of the goddess, effortlessly sure of sustaining her balance in the rhythm of propulsion.'[8] Much critical attention has been devoted to Botticelli's famous painting, all of it presupposing that this work is to be valued highly.

I have spoken of descriptions supporting interpretations, of lower-level interpretative statements supporting higher-level ones, and of critics arguing for evaluations by means of interpretations. It still remains unexplained what kind of support and what kind of argument is involved. The outlines of the problem may become clearer if we consider two different ways in which we may disagree with a critic. At the beginning of this discussion I focused on the possibility of accepting an interpretation but refusing to agree with an evaluation. I considered the case where I find *Waiting for Godot* a good play and you do not. You may accept my interpretative points about Beckett's use of language, his exploitation of a situation, and his treatment of dramatic conventions but object that, nevertheless, the play fails to meet other criteria for a good play. I say these criteria are irrelevant to this particular play but you disagree. The problem here is not just that we agree on an interpretation but disagree on the evaluation. We are disagreeing over the relative importance of different factors in the interpretation. To get you to agree with me I have to persuade you of the importance of my criteria for this play's worth. I have to persuade you that when you see the play the features which stand out are the ones I consider valuable. I may even try to persuade you that the lack of structure, rather than detracting from the overall effect, contributes to it since it helps us to see that the life of the two tramps, and perhaps all human life, lacks structure. I have to ask you to go and see the play with my interpretation and my evaluation in mind. Argument in the abstract will only take us so far. The acid test for both interpretation and evaluation of a literary work is renewed contact with the text, or, in the case of drama, with performance. We must ask, 'Can the play be seen in this way?' 'Can the novel or poem be read in this way?'

Before taking this point further let us consider a second, more common way in which we may disagree with a critic. Let us return to Traversi's account of the masque in Act IV of *The Tempest* quoted earlier. There are a number of points at which we might question Traversi's detailed interpretation. We might argue that the masque *is* necessary as a ratification of the betrothal of Ferdinand and Miranda precisely because the scenes in which they acknowledge their love for one another and Prospero gives his approval are, as Traversi admits, brief. We might object that other parts of the masque such as the opening conversation between the spirits representing Ceres and Iris are as important as the song. We might question what is meant by the claim that, 'this interlude . . . belongs more to the structural unity of the play than to its intimate poetic sensibility'. The masque is quite as much an interlude in structural terms as in terms of theme and 'poetic sensibility'. Indeed, its relevance to the play comes from its themes rather than its sudden insertion into the structure.

If we offer objections of this kind we are not accepting an interpretation while refusing to accept the consequent evaluation. Instead we are refusing to accept Traversi's interpretation of the details of the scene. We refuse because when we read or see the play the masque does not strike us as it strikes Traversi. Once again the crucial question is, 'Can this part of the play be seen in this way?' Similarly, I must be able to see the pose of Botticelli's Venus as weightless and effortless before I can assent to Levey's praise of the painting's harmonious composition. Before I can accept a critic's interpretation of a piece of music I need to listen to the music again and see if I can hear in it what the critic hears.

When we are dealing with a play the acid test will be seeing it in performance, not just reading it in the study. There is a complication here which may shed further light on the nature of critical interpretation. We speak not only of the interpretation of literature by critics but also of the interpretation of a play by a producer and by actors. The plays of Shakespeare, for example, are interpreted in this sense. They are put on in settings of the producer's own devising, in eighteenth-century dress, in Edwardian dress, or in modern dress. In putting on, say, *The Tempest* in modern dress the producer is suggesting a certain interpretation of the play, suggesting that the themes explored in *The Tempest* are relevant to modern times and modern society as well as to the fictional and fantastic society of the play and to Shakespeare's own time. The actor's interpretation of a part may well colour our perception even more than the producer's interpretation of the play. Different actors may play a complex dramatic character such as Hamlet in quite different ways.

Interpretation in this sense is common to all the performing arts. The conductor and the players interpret pieces of music, singers interpret songs, dancers interpret ballets. Just as we may disagree with the interpretation of a play offered by a critic, so we may disagree with the interpretation offered in a particular performance. At first it may seem that we disagree simply because we do not care for the interpretation offered: we do not like Shakespeare in modern dress, or we had always thought of Hamlet as only feigning madness and not really mad, or we prefer the soloist in Max Bruch's Violin Concerto to make less use of tempo rubato. Here we seem to be back in the realms of subjective preference. However, when challenged we are likely to offer reasons for our disagreement. We may argue that a modern setting is inappropriate for *The Tempest* because it makes Prospero's magic incredible and cannot satisfactorily accommodate the fantastic figures of Ariel and Caliban. We may point to passages in the text of *Hamlet* which suggest that Hamlet's madness is only feigned. We may point out how too much use of tempo rubato by the soloist breaks up the structure of Bruch's Violin Concerto. In each case we shall be appealing to the text of the work, or its musical equivalent, to support our view and to disqualify what we regard as an inappropriate interpretation.

In response the critic or producer or performer who supports the interpretation we disagree with will in turn point to elements in the text which support their view and tell against ours. If an aesthetically valuable work is one which is rich in possibilities of interpretation it might seem that the more valuable a work is, the more various will be the interpretations that can be given of it. There might be only one interpretation of a Barbara Cartland novel but there will be a number of interpretations of a Jane Austen novel or a Shakespeare play. There will be more than one way of giving a good performance of Max Bruch's Violin Concerto. Even if we say that all the interpretations of a work are admissible, we must acknowledge that it may not be possible to read or perform the work in accordance with all the suggested interpretations at once. Hamlet cannot be both genuinely mad and feigning madness. The soloist in Bruch's concerto cannot make much and little use of tempo rubato at the same time.

When I have imagined critical disagreements such as the disagreement over *Waiting for Godot* to illustrate my argument so far, I have spoken in terms of one person trying to persuade another. In the last chapter I stressed the importance of personal experience of works of art and in this chapter too I have stressed that the final stage in persuading others to share my view of a work is to get them to see, hear, or read it as I do. When we consider the variety of interpretations that have been offered of many works of art and consider also that differing interpretations can lead to widely differing evaluations, it might appear that the claim of aesthetic judgements to universal validity is wholly spurious. The way in which I express my judgement that *Waiting for Godot* is a good play may indeed suggest that I think you ought to react to the play as I do but perhaps all I am trying to do in expressing myself in this way is persuade you to share my reaction. Perhaps aesthetic disputes are resolved by persuasion rather than rational argument and the apparent attempt to justify an aesthetic judgement is simply a method of persuasion. On such a view the apparatus of critical description and interpretation is not superfluous but it is a tool of persuasion rather than a means of rational justification.

If the critic is really a hidden persuader, there may be no limit to the power of his rhetoric. Perhaps any interpretation of a work is possible and any evaluation too. Perhaps we only think an interpretation or an evaluation wrong because we have not yet been persuaded of it. In time if we come to see the work the way our opponent does then we shall come to agree with him.[9]

It is all too easy to leap from the evident fact that many works of art are susceptible of more than one interpretation, and the recognition that different interpretations of a work may conflict with one another, to the wild claim that there is no limit to the possible interpretations. Yet experience suggests that while there may be no one right interpretation of a work there can be wrong interpretations, that we cannot be persuaded of just *anything*, that some critical assessments can be shown to be mistaken. If this is correct we would expect there to be some kind of standard for critical procedure and that critics who fail to meet this standard fail to provide justification for their views.

The merit of describing the critic's activity as persuasion is that such a model takes full account of an important fact: the critic does not convey information but tries to modify or alter our attitudes towards works of art. (Of course, critics may also convey information: for example, writers on literature may tell us about an author's life, about when a work was first published, or about different readings in different manuscripts or editions of a text, but this is not part of their activity as literary critics offering aesthetic judgements.) However, the implied contrast between persuasion and rational justification is misleading. There are different methods of persuasion, and reasoned argument plays a role in some but not in others. The advertiser who tries to persuade us to buy a popular novel by ensuring that its name appears frequently in the media and that the book is prominently displayed in shops is employing a different kind of persuasion from the critic who tries to get us to value the book by suggesting we read it with our minds alert to certain features of the text. What we need is an account of the method of persuasion employed by the critic. How does he bring us to see the text in the way that he does, to read it as he reads it?

We have already seen that description, interpretation, and evaluation are intertwined in criticism and that evaluations must be argued for by means of interpretation and description. I do not mean to suggest that there will be a one-to-one correspondence between an evaluation and a particular interpretation. *The Tempest* may be a good play under more than one interpretation but *some* interpretation must be offered if the claim that it is a good play is to be borne out, and the interpretation offered must be justified in accordance with normal critical procedure. Interpretations are justified by pointing to features of the text. Interpretations will differ in drawing attention to different features and can initially be assessed according to the amount of textual evidence there is for them. 'Features of a text' may cover a wide range. Style, plot, theme, and characterization may all be appealed to in support of an interpretation. In the end, with a literary text, the basis of all such features lies in the words used so that justifiable interpretations must appeal to actual passages of the text. It is no good saying that Hamlet is depicted as only feigning madness without pointing to the words in the play which so depict him. An interpretation that depends on only a few lines in a play will be less convincing than an interpretation which can be backed up by passages taken from many points in the play. I said that the best test of an interpretation was whether the text could be read in that way. For a text to be read under a certain interpretation we must be able to see it all in the light of that interpretation. That will be easy where there is ample textual evidence for the interpretation, difficult where the interpretation depends on very limited textual evidence. Similarly, an interpretation of a

1. Constable, *The Hay Wain* (reproduced by courtesy of the Trustees, The National Gallery, London)

2. Uccello, *The Battle of San Romano* (reproduced by courtesy of the Trustees, The National Gallery, London)

3. Botticelli, *The Birth of Venus* (photo: Mansell Collection)

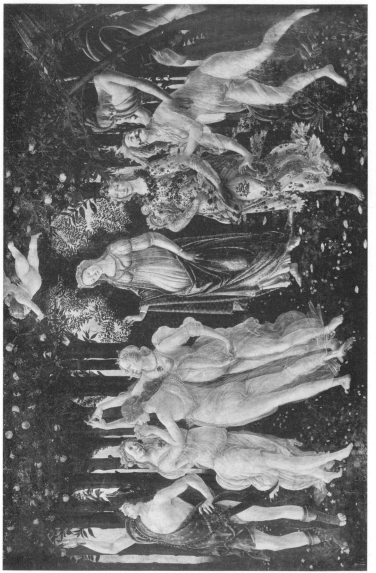

4. Botticelli, *Primavera* (photo: Mansell Collection)

painting or a piece of music is justified by pointing to features of the work and the more features of the work support the interpretation offered, the stronger that interpretation becomes.

As well as considering how much textual evidence there is in favour of a given interpretation we must also see whether anything in the text goes against it. If numerous passages in the text are incompatible with the interpretation offered then it will be hard to read the text in its light. If the evidence against is sparse or non-existent, the interpretation gains in strength. Again the same applies to interpretations of visual art and of music. There too we must see whether anything in the work tells against the interpretation offered. Simply counting the number of passages or features which tell for or against an interpretation is not enough. Two other factors are relevant: the dispersal of such passages or features through the work and their importance. The first of these factors presents no problems. Interpretations based on evidence scattered throughout a work are clearly more convincing than those based on evidence concentrated in one small portion of it. However, the second factor, the importance of a passage or a feature, is itself a matter requiring critical judgement. It is not something which can be decided simply by inspecting the work without any preconceptions. We can best discuss how such importance may be assessed by further examination of critical disagreements.

Let us consider cases where there are two or more conflicting interpretations of a literary text, each supported by an equal weight of evidence drawn from the text. The interpretations will differ in either or both of two ways. The conflicting interpretations may appeal to different features of the text because they regard different features as important. Alternatively, they may appeal to the same features of the text but understand those features differently. I shall start by examining the second kind of case.

William Blake's famous poem, 'The Tyger', has been the subject of a number of different interpretations. In 1954 Kathleen Raine published an article arguing that the tiger for Blake is 'a symbol of competitive, predacious selfhood' and is to be regarded as evil. In her view the answer to the poem's final question, 'Did he who made the Lamb make thee?' is a firm 'No'. Among her evidence is Blake's use of the word 'forests' in the second line,

'In the forests of the night'. She argues that 'forest' in Blake always refers to 'the natural, "fallen" world', a world created in Blake's view by a secondary, evil creator, distinct from Christ, the creator of the Lamb. Ten years later E.D.Hirsch argued for a quite different interpretation of the poem. In Hirsch's view 'The Tyger' 'celebrates the holiness of tigerness'. In this poem the 'ferocity and destructiveness' of the tiger are transfigured. Terrible as the tiger is, it is also beautiful. The same God created both tiger and lamb, in a creation which transcends human good and evil. Hirsch too appeals to the word 'forests' but understands that word in quite a different way. ' "Forests",' he says, 'suggests tall straight forms, a world that for all its terror has the orderliness of the tiger's stripes or Blake's perfectly balanced verses.'[10]

This kind of example is striking and in a way disturbing since it appears to suggest that the very features of the text itself are unstable. In a sense Kathleen Raine and E.D.Hirsch are *not* appealing to the same feature. The word 'forests' means different things to each of these two critics and it could be argued that this kind of critical disagreement collapses into the first kind, where conflicting interpretations appeal to different features of the text. There is, it seems, no one feature of the text constituted by the word 'forests'. If, however, there are no such things as stable 'features of the text' then the possibility of weighing up one interpretation against another collapses too and we are back in a situation where a clever critic might persuade us of any interpretation whatever, understanding the words of the text in any way he or she pleased.

However, we need not fall back as far as this. In fact disagreements like the one between Kathleen Raine and E.D.Hirsch are not very common because most writers make it clearer than Blake does what they mean by their words. Blake writes obscure, symbolic poetry which can be understood on a number of different levels. Perhaps there *is* a sense in which the features of Blake's text are unstable but it does not follow that all features of all texts are unstable. Moreover, we should notice that the example as given concerns the interpretation of one word only. Neither Raine's nor Hirsch's interpretation rests on that word alone. Raine produces a wealth of other evidence from Gnostic, Hermetic, and cabbalistic texts, which she argues were known to

Blake, and from other passages in Blake's own works. Hirsch's interpretation rests partly on a detailed discussion of the imagery, rhythms, and syntax of the whole poem. In addition it is backed up by a general argument that Blake's attitude to the natural world changed in the course of his life so that it is a mistake to interpret all Blake's poems in terms of any one system. That argument in turn is supported by evidence from Blake's manuscripts as well as his published works. The question is not what individual pieces of evidence a critic appeals to but his total web of evidence. It would, admittedly, be puzzling if two critics offered conflicting interpretations based on the same total corpus of evidence. In such a rare case we would simply have to say the work in question was radically ambiguous, it could be read in either way. Both interpretations would be justified.

It is much more common for interpretations to differ by regarding different features as important. My imaginary case of a disagreement over *Waiting for Godot* was a critical disagreement of this kind. Here we must take account of profound disagreements between critics of different schools. If a critic holds some general theory of how texts should be interpreted, that theory will determine in advance what features of a text he or she regards as important. A structuralist, for example, will look for repeated thematic patterns in an author's work and will often concern himself not just with an individual text but with a group of texts. So Tzvetan Todorov picks on the theme of the quest for an essentially absent secret as the most important feature of Henry James's short stories and justifies his interpretation of those stories by pointing out how such a quest constantly recurs in different forms.[11] A quite different, Freudian interpretation of James's most celebrated short story, *The Turn of the Screw*, was offered by Edmund Wilson. He picked out passages in the text which associate the ghosts seen by the governess with Freudian symbols. So Wilson regards it as significant that the male ghost first appears on a tower, a phallic symbol, while the female ghost first appears beside the water of a lake, a Freudian symbol of birth and so more generally of female sexuality and motherhood.[12] A Marxist critic will regard as important still other features of a text from those which catch the attention of the structuralist or the Freudian. He or she will look for connections between a text and the ways of thinking, the 'ideology', of the society in which it was created. So George Lukács, for example, interpreted the nineteenth-century realistic novel as reflecting the nature of nineteenth-century capitalism. He praised Balzac's novel, *Les Paysans*, on the grounds that Balzac, despite his own reactionary political views, in fact brings out clearly in the novel the conflict between three social classes, the landowners, the bourgeois capitalists, and the peasants. To support his interpretation Lukács picked out passages in the novel which stress the existence of such a conflict.[13]

Critics who belong to a particular school may well be less concerned to persuade others of their interpretation of one particular text than to persuade them to accept their general theory of what is important in texts. If the theory is accepted, the individual interpretations will follow readily enough. If we are not committed to any such theory we seem to be left with trying to assess the amount and weight of evidence for a given interpretation by seeing if the text can be read in a certain way. Interpretations which rest on very sparse or limited evidence can be ruled out but we will still be left with a lot of others. Like an actor trying out different ways of playing a role we can try reading *The Turn of the Screw* first in a structuralist way and then in a Freudian way. On one interpretation one set of features will be important, on another interpretation another set. Different interpretations may produce different evaluations. A novel might be very bad from a Marxist point of view, very good from a structuralist point of view. Even if we admit the rarity of cases where two critics offer exactly the same textual evidence for conflicting interpretations, the much more frequent cases where critics regard different features of a text as important suggest that there is no one correct interpretation and evaluation of a literary work. We seem to be left with little firm ground to stand on, still open to persuasion by any critic who comes along with a good haul of textual evidence well deployed in support of his interpretation and evaluation.

The same problem can confront us in the other arts. While Michael Levey regards the pose of Botticelli's Venus as weightless, effortless, and symbolic of the perfect harmony of the composition, Edgar Wind, in an allegorical interpretation of the painting, claims that, 'The goddess's own posture, that of the classical *Venus pudica*, expresses the dual nature of love, both sensuous and chaste . . . '[14] How are we to decide which interpretation of Venus' pose is correct, which way we should look at the painting?

We may return at this point to another kind of aesthetic judgement, the aesthetic appreciation of nature. Different scenes in nature may be appreciated from different points of view and spectators may differ in the features of a scene which they see as important. In Chapter 5 I considered a situation in which two people are looking at a landscape of farms, some cultivated land, and rolling hills. One finds it peaceful while to the other it presents a scene of busy activity. I said there that these spectators would be concentrating on different features of the landscape. In the case of nature we as beholders have considerable freedom to select our point of view. Have we just as much freedom when we contemplate works of art? In Chapter 5 I said that the artist, by choosing which features to bring into prominence, can to some extent control how we see or hear the work and how we react. In this chapter I have kept the artist on one side and have been considering the critic's use of evidence from the work. In fact critics often appeal to a number of other considerations in support of their views. They may appeal to other works in the same genre or to other works by the same person. They may also appeal to the expectations of the original audience or to the artist's intentions. Attempts to limit the range of permissible interpretations of a work of art characteristically make some such criterion outside the work itself the test of a correct interpretation. In the next chapter we must examine whether one interpretation, or one group of interpretations, of a work can be given such privileged status. In particular, conformity with the artist's intentions appears to provide a stringent criterion of the correctness of an interpretation. I shall concentrate on that topic but it will be helpful to place it in the context of other attempts to make an external criterion the test of a correct interpretation.

7
Intentions and expectations

Our discussion of the critic's procedure failed to resolve the question whether one interpretation or group of interpretations of a work of art can be picked out as correct. Some interpretations may be ruled out as insufficiently supported by the text of a literary work or the details of a painting or piece of music but the text itself will not provide us with any guarantee of correctness; moreover, for many works we will be faced with a number of interpretations, some conflicting with one another but all grounded in the text. In fact, as I said at the end of the last chapter, critics often appeal to considerations outside the text to provide additional support for their views. I mentioned four kinds of consideration: other works in the same genre, other works by the same person, the expectations of the original audience, and the artist's intentions. These four may be reduced to two as we shall see if we examine them a little further.

To say that critics may appeal to other works in the same genre in support of an interpretation is an oversimplification. Critics often appeal not only to considerations of genre but to a whole range of considerations drawn from artistic form and convention. For example, when J. B. Leishman discusses Milton's 'Lycidas', he not only relates the poem to its classical predecessors, poems by Moschus, Theocritus, and Virgil, and to the English pastoral tradition as exemplified by Sidney, Spenser, Shakespeare, and others. He also compares it with the other contemporary poems written to commemorate Edward King whose death occasioned the writing of 'Lycidas'. Leishman's concern is not so much to show Milton's indebtedness to the literary tradition as to display Milton's originality in his use of that tradition. He does this partly by comparing Milton's poem with the more pedestrian efforts of his contemporaries and partly by detailed examination of the way in which Milton has adapted and transformed phrases and images previously used by others.[1] Our appreciation of 'Lycidas' is enhanced when we know something of the literary tradition in which Milton was working and so can see how he innovates within that tradition. Similarly, our appreciation of the paintings of Giotto is enhanced if we relate them to medieval art and compare them with the more traditional but equally fine work of his contemporary Simone Martini. And our appreciation of the music of Vaughan Williams is enhanced if we relate it to the English church music and folk music which influenced him and compare it with the music of his contemporary Elgar.

Critics may also appeal to other works by the same person. Consider again the passage quoted in the last chapter drawn from Derek Traversi's discussion of *The Tempest*. Traversi points to a similarity between the theme of the masque in *The Tempest* and 'a similar union' in *The Winter's Tale* (the union of Perdita and Florizel). When he criticizes the masque as belonging 'more to the structural unity of the play than to its intimate poetic sensibility' he describes it as in this respect 'like its not altogether dissimilar predecessor in *Cymbeline*'. The assumption here is that just as similarities between works in the same literary genre may be illuminating, so similarities between works by the same author may be illuminating. In the book from which my example was drawn, *Shakespeare: The Last Phase*, Traversi is concerned with Shakespeare's last plays and regards all the plays written at the same period of Shakespeare's life as casting light on one another. He refers to the 'continuous development of theme and treatment which makes it impossible to regard any of [Shakespeare's plays] as mere isolated masterpieces' and of the four plays discussed in the book, *Pericles, Cymbeline, The Winter's Tale*, and *The Tempest*, he says, 'That these comedies, apparently produced in the space of some two years, between 1609 and 1611, form a close artistic unity is revealed clearly in the pattern discernible in their respective plots.'[2] Similarly, critics of visual art and music may use other works by the same artist or the same composer to illuminate one another.

Such parallels with other works in the same genre or other works by the same person will never afford conclusive proof of the correctness of an interpretation since, despite the similarities between works of art, each one is unique. We have already seen in the last chapter that proof of this kind is not attainable in criticism. Such considerations can, however, support a critic's view by helping us to read or see or hear a work in the light of a particular interpretation. Parallels with other works support an interpretation only if they do indeed enhance our appreciation of the work.

In many Shakespeare plays there are scenes where characters indulge in passages of punning and verbal sparring. The Fools in the comedies, such as Feste in *Twelfth Night* or Touchstone in *As You Like It*, are particularly given to this. Such scenes may be rather boring to a modern audience but we are told that the Elizabethans enjoyed them. This feature of Shakespeare's plays is explained by appeal to the original audience's expectations. When we try to understand and appreciate works of the past or works from a foreign culture we are often trying to put ourselves in the position of the original audience. (I shall use 'the audience' throughout this chapter as a convenient shorthand for the readers of literature, the audience of music, drama, and dance, and the spectators of painting, sculpture, architecture, and the other visual arts.) To put ourselves in the position of the original audience we must find out all sorts of things about them—not only what they liked in literature, music, and art but their social background, their ways of thinking, their attitudes to religion, sex, and politics, their attitudes to both the past and the future, their attitudes to foreigners and to their fellow-countrymen. This is why a proper appreciation of Aeschylean tragedy requires an understanding of classical Greek culture and society, a proper appreciation of Bach's organ music requires an understanding of eighteenth-century German Protestantism, and a proper appreciation of the art of Giotto or Botticelli requires an understanding of the world of the Italian Renaissance.

What we are seeking to achieve is not so much an exact re-creation of what any particular member of the work's original audience experienced as a general understanding of what it would have been like to be one of the original audience. We are seeking an ideal, in two senses of that word. It is an ideal in the sense that 'the expectations of the original audience' is an abstraction not identical with the reactions of any one member of that audience. Although documents which tell us how a particular work was received when first played, published, produced, or exhibited will be valuable, even a diary kept by the most acute and precise contemporary critic will not include everything we would wish to take into account. Many of the assumptions and attitudes we discover when we study classical Greece, or eighteenth-century Germany, or the Italian Renaissance were not consciously formulated by the people who lived in those societies. Future historians will formulate the assumptions and attitudes of our own society more clearly than we ourselves can do. The general understanding that we seek is also an ideal in the sense that we can never fully achieve it. However much we know about classical Greece or eighteenth-century Germany or the Italian Renaissance it will always be possible to discover more, we shall continually be having to adjust our picture of what it was like to be an ancient Greek or a German in the time of Bach or a Renaissance Italian. We may be able to formulate some Greek assumptions and attitudes more clearly than the most self-aware ancient Greek could ever do, but we can never quite recapture the Greek's experience. Yet our efforts to recapture it are not wasted, for, paradoxically, we can get closer and closer even though we can never attain our goal.

Although we can never fully share the expectations of the original audience, such understanding as we have attained can be used to support critical interpretations. If someone claimed to find references in Shakespeare to nuclear warfare, we could rule them out as incomprehensible to Elizabethan and Jacobean audiences. Features that puzzle us, such as the Shakespearian scenes of punning and wordplay which I mentioned, can often be explained when we take the expectations of the original audience into account. Finally, we can use our knowledge of these expectations to argue for interpretations, maintaining, for example, that Prospero's magic in *The Tempest* is to be taken seriously because a belief in magic was still common when the play was written, in the reign of James I: women were still burnt as witches and King James himself wrote a book on witchcraft and magic.

Among an audience's expectations of a work of art are expectations concerned with artistic forms and conventions. The Greeks of the fifth century BC would expect a chorus in a tragedy. Shakespeare's contemporaries would expect a Fool in a comedy. Mozart's contemporaries would expect harpsichord music to be played with trills and grace-notes. Giotto's contemporaries would expect saints to be painted with haloes. When a critic appeals to considerations of artistic form and convention this is in fact yet another kind of appeal to the audience's expectations. Of course not all members of the original audience will have been equally well informed on artistic matters. The appeal to the expectations of the original audience is an appeal not to any actual audience but to an idealized abstraction. In this ideal original audience we suppose a full knowledge of prevailing artistic conventions, such as only some of the actual audience will have had.

Our own response to works of art from the past may be modified by our knowledge of what has happened in art since. The refrain of Spenser's 'Prothalamion', 'Sweet Thames, run softly, till I end my song', may read differently to us once we are familiar with its occurrence in Section III of T.S.Eliot's *The Waste Land*. Eliot himself argued that new works, introduced into the tradition, modify the works of the past.[3] Yet if we regard the expectations of the original audience as providing a criterion by which to judge a critical interpretation we must say that however much fun it is to read Spenser with Eliot in mind that is not the right way to read him. We may in practice find it very difficult to read Spenser without having Eliot in mind but if we want a justifiable interpretation of Spenser, that is what we should strive to do. The same applies to works from a foreign culture. It is no good regarding a Japanese haiku as a kind of abbreviated Western lyric poem. If we do that the haiku may seem puzzling and unsuccessful or it may seem a charming gem but either way we are not really understanding it. To understand it we must learn about Japanese literary conventions and try to read the poem as a Japanese would read it. I am not saying that we cannot find amusement and interest in reading Spenser with Eliot in mind or that we cannot get anything out of a haiku without knowing about Japanese culture. What I am saying is that if we are aiming at justifiable interpretation then we must inform ourselves about the period and the society in which the work of art originated.

We saw in Chapter 6 that the relationship between interpretation and evaluation is complex. Many artists have been valued more highly by later ages than in their own lifetime even though their contemporaries could understand their works well enough. A greater problem for my present argument is presented by works which are not even understood when they first appear. Artists may be 'ahead of their time' in producing boldly innovative works which initially baffle audiences. I said that in appealing to the original audience's expectations the critic is appealing to an ideal, not to any actual audience. Are we then to say that an ideal audience would never have had any difficulty in appreciating Cubist painting or 'stream of consciousness' fiction? This answer is too easy, for it belies the facts of aesthetic experience. As I noted in Chapter 2, we may come to regard as especially valuable works which cannot be comprehended without imaginative effort. The audience's expectations are not the sole criterion of justifiable interpretation. The successful artist plays with his audience's expectations, satisfying some of them while disappointing others, using his work to modify existing expectations and create new ones. This brings us to the fourth kind of consideration outside the text to which a critic may appeal, the artist's intentions.

Explicit statements of intention distinct from the work are not very common but critics often appeal to evidence from which the artist's intentions are inferred. Some of this evidence may come from the text itself. So one might argue that Shakespeare intended Prospero's magic in *The Tempest* to be taken seriously because everybody in the play takes it seriously. Some of the other kinds of evidence for what an artist had in mind are used by Kathleen Raine and E. D. Hirsch in the dispute about the interpretation of Blake's 'The Tyger' discussed in the last chapter. Raine supports her interpretation of Blake's attitude to the natural world by referring to Gnostic, Hermetic, and cabbalistic texts which she argues were known to Blake. She also cites other passages in Blake's own works. Hirsch supports his different interpretation not only by appealing to other passages in Blake's published works but also by adducing evidence from Blake's manuscripts.

We can see from reflection on this example that appeal to other works by the same person is not after all a distinct type of consideration. It is appeal to one kind of evidence for the artist's intentions. When we refer to the artist's intentions we are assuming that a work or a group of works has been produced by one person with a consistent set of attitudes and beliefs. When Hirsch argues that the attitude to the natural world in 'The Tyger' differs from the attitude expressed in Blake's earlier poem, 'The Lamb', he argues that Blake's attitude changed. Where we find inconsistencies between different works by the same artist or, even worse, within one work, various critical strategies are possible. We may argue that the inconsistencies are not inconsistencies at all if they are seen in a different way—some further interpretation may be possible which embraces them all or the artist may have adopted different personae in different places. Alternatively we may say that the artist has not achieved what he or she set out to do so that the inconsistencies are the result of accident. A third possibility is to regard the inconsistencies as the product not of unachieved intentions but of inconsistent intentions. In this case we will appeal to a change of mind by the artist, or perhaps to a conflict between the artist's conscious intentions and his or her subconscious assumptions. If we do not adopt any of these strategies we are likely to abandon the notion that one person produced the work or works under consideration. If the inconsistencies are in an individual work, perhaps that work is the result of a collaboration. If the inconsistencies are between works ascribed to the same artist, perhaps they are not all in fact by that artist.

Suppose, however, that we discovered that the works of Shakespeare had not been produced by a human being at all. They were produced neither by Shakespeare nor by Bacon but by monkeys playing with a typewriter. Talk of the artist's intentions would then become irrelevant. So would talk of the expectations of the original audience since such talk assumes that a work has been deliberately produced by one or more conscious human beings for presentation to an audience. We might still admire what those monkeys had produced but we could interpret it as we pleased, free from any critical constraints. Some structuralist and post-structuralist critics regard all interpretations of a work as equally justified. With perfect consistency these critics deny that the artist's intentions have any relevance to criticism. In doing so they are ignoring an essential fact about art. Works of art differ from natural objects precisely in being produced by a particular person, or by particular people, at a particular time, in a particular society. They have authors and points of origin. These two factors form the basis of critics' appeals to evidence other than that offered by the text itself and it is here that we must look for further justification of interpretations. The two factors are interconnected since it is normally part of an artist's intention that a work be presented to an audience and he or she must write in such a way that an audience can in the end understand the work. Even artists who are ahead of their time conform to some conventions accepted by their audience, while abandoning or modifying others. The assumption that a work is written to be understood forms part of an audience's expectations of a work. Moreover, many assumptions about artistic forms and many moral, social, and political attitudes will be shared by an artist and his or her contemporary audience. When we learn about the culture and society of fifth-century Greece we learn not only about the expectations of Aeschylus' audience but about assumptions and attitudes Aeschylus himself is likely to have shared. When we learn about the culture and society of Renaissance Italy we learn not only about the expectations of those who first looked at Giotto's painting but about assumptions and attitudes shared by Giotto himself.

The relevance of the author's intentions to literary criticism has been hotly debated. In what follows I shall concentrate on intentions but we shall see that a proper understanding of intention in art involves understanding of the audience's expectations also. Forty years ago a celebrated attack on appeal to the author's intentions in literary criticism was launched by W. K. Wimsatt and M. C. Beardsley.[4] Wimsatt and Beardsley called their article 'The Intentional Fallacy' and declared roundly 'the design or intention of the author is neither available nor desirable as a standard for judging the success of a work of literary art'.[5] Here the reference to 'judging success' suggests a concern with evaluation but when they go on to discuss examples of the 'intentional fallacy' exhibited by critics it becomes clear that they have interpretation also in mind. In that article they do not clearly distinguish between the two. Wimsatt and Beardsley are right that an author's intentions do not offer any criterion by which to judge the *success* of a work. I may set out to write a masterpiece and produce something quite worthless. The interesting issue, on which much of the subsequent debate has focused, is the relevance of the author's intentions to interpretation and here Wimsatt and Beardsley are in the end mistaken. To see just why they are mistaken we must examine their position more closely.

Wimsatt and Beardsley say that the author's intention is 'neither available nor desirable'. Their argument for the undesirability of appeals to intention rests largely on claims that only 'internal' evidence should be regarded as relevant to literary criticism, that is, only evidence drawn from the text of the work under discussion. When the article was written its authors were reacting sharply against types of literary criticism which offered extensive discussion of an author's life and possible state of mind when writing a work while failing to look closely at the details of the text. We have approached the problem in a different way. In Chapter 6 I laid stress on the critic's concern with the details of the text and on the need for a critical interpretation to be supported by evidence drawn from the text. The question we are now considering is not whether criticism based on knowledge of the author's intentions should supersede criticism based on details of the text. Nor is it a question about the use of literature as evidence for an author's biography. Inferences about events in an author's life or about an author's state of mind drawn from literary works are notoriously unsound. Attempted reconstructions of the course of Catullus' love affair with Lesbia based on his poems can never be more than speculation since there is a dearth of other evidence. We cannot know when Catullus is writing a poem based on a real situation and when he is writing a poem based on an imaginary situation or on an exaggerated version of a real situation. The same applies to attempts to reconstruct Shakespeare's relationship with the Dark Lady of the Sonnets or with Mr W.H. In any case such attempts at biographical reconstruction are not literary criticism. They lead away from literary works towards speculations about their creators. The use of literature as biographical evidence should, however, be distinguished from the use of biographical evidence, including evidence of the author's intentions, to illuminate literature.

I would agree with Wimsatt and Beardsley that the critic should begin with a close study of the literary text. The problem is what to do when the text gives rise to conflicting interpretations. Can appeal to the author's intentions help to determine which interpretation can best be justified? If we want a way of deciding between conflicting interpretations, a way which gives due weight to the fact that a work is written by a particular person, or by particular people, at a particular time, in a particular society, then evidence of the author's intentions does appear desirable. Is it available?

Wimsatt and Beardsley define what they mean by 'intention' as 'what he intended', that is, 'design or plan in the author's mind'.[6] This they regard as in principle unavailable since we can never know for certain what is going on in someone else's mind. The root of Wimsatt and Beardsley's mistake lies in their assumption that to understand an author's intentions we have to gain access to what was going on in his or her mind. 'Intention' is not a term confined to the discussion of works of art. It is freely used in two other spheres, both of which are important for the discussion of art. We also speak of 'intention' in relation to action and in relation to language. The intention with which an action has been performed is of the greatest moral and legal importance. Intention makes the difference between taking something by mistake and stealing it, between manslaughter and murder. When we make moral judgements and legal decisions we certainly regard knowledge of an agent's intentions as not only desirable but available. In the sphere of language intention is closely connected with meaning. When we speak we intend to communicate the meaning of our words and we assume that that intention is known to our hearers. The successful use of language as a means of communication depends on the assumption that knowledge of speakers' intentions is both desirable and available.

Actions, language, and works of art are all produced by human beings and some of the philosophical discussion of intention in relation to both action and language can usefully be applied to intention in relation to works of art.[7] Actions are normally assumed to be intentional unless there is reason to think otherwise. If I bump into somebody in a crowd that person turns round and glares because he assumes that I knew what I was doing, and intentionally, in my determination to move forward, bumped into him. He will be mollified if I then excuse myself and say, 'I'm sorry, I didn't mean to do that' or 'I'm sorry, that was an accident'. The unintentional or the accidental is the exception, not the rule. The same is true of language. Suppose I make a bad pun and my hearer responds with a grimace. This response assumes that I intended my pun, that I was trying to make my hearer laugh but I have a rather feeble sense of humour. The hearer's reaction changes when I say, 'I'm sorry, that was unintentional. I didn't realize it was a pun.'

Actions can be intentional without being preceded by conscious deliberation. If I am going on an exceptional day's outing I probably do engage in some conscious planning. If I intend to catch a train at 10 a.m., then I must leave the house at 9 a.m. and to be able to do that I must get up at 7.30 a.m. and to make sure I wake up in time I had better set the alarm clock. I am unlikely, however, to have thought out every detail of my actions in advance. I may decide on the spur of the moment to leave the breakfast dishes unwashed but I am not leaving them unwashed unintentionally. If I am simply setting off for my daily work at the same time as usual I may not make any conscious plans at all. Yet I get up when the alarm goes off, eat breakfast, and leave the house at the usual time. I do not do these things unintentionally, even though I have not consciously deliberated about them. In either case an observer would infer that I was acting intentionally from the fact that my behaviour followed a coherent pattern which appeared to be directed towards a particular aim, catching the train or arriving at work on time.

The same is true of language. If I am going to make a formal after-dinner speech then I engage in conscious deliberation. I think out what I am going to say, plan the order of topics, and note down some witty turns of phrase which I intend to use. If I am going to converse with somebody important whom I have not met before, I may likewise devote some thought to good conversational gambits and ways of expressing myself. The fact that I do not plan the speech or the conversation in every detail does not make my impromptu elaborations of my previously planned sentences unintentional. If, on the other hand, I am chatting with people I know well I do not plan in advance what I will say at all. Yet my conversation is not unintentional and is not regarded as such by my hearers. In either case my hearers will only attribute lack of intention to me if there is some sudden lapse from my normal pattern of linguistic behaviour: I suddenly make a bad pun although I am not given to punning or I make a tactless remark although I am usually quite tactful.

Actions and language are assumed to be intentional if they follow a coherent pattern. If we seek the intention *with which* an action was performed or a statement was made, we must study the pattern into which it appears to fit. So my getting out of bed when the alarm goes off makes sense as an intentional action if seen in the context of the series of actions which leads to my arriving at work on time. If we are puzzled about the intention with which something was done we may seek an explanation from the agent or the speaker. A guest, staying in my house and unused to my habits, might be puzzled about my laying the table for breakfast at 10 o'clock at night. If asked why I am doing this, I will explain that it is to save time next morning, to make sure I leave the house in time to get to work. Such cases are the exception, not the rule. Most of our knowledge about the intentions of other people comes from inference based on observed patterns of behaviour, not from explicit declarations of intention.

Like actions and language, works of art are assumed to be the products of intention unless there is reason to think otherwise and just as actions and language can be intentionally produced without being the product of conscious deliberation, so can works of art. In art too intentions are inferred from the observation of coherent patterns. I said earlier that some of the evidence for an artist's intentions may come from the text of the work itself. This is just what we should expect if we take seriously the point that a work of art is intentionally produced. If we ask, 'Did Shakespeare intend us to take Prospero's magic in *The Tempest* seriously?', the first place to look for an answer to the question is the text of *The Tempest*. We must ask whether other features of the text, such as the attitudes towards Prospero exhibited by the other characters, suggest that the magic is to be taken seriously. We saw in Chapter 4 that formalist critics often seek to find unity, coherence, and order in works of art. Although formalism is frequently associated with a firm rejection of any reference to the artist's intentions, in looking for order and coherence in a work the formalist is seeking the kind of pattern characteristic of an intentionally produced object.[8]

When we try to discover the intention with which another person's action was performed we seek to find a pattern in a whole series of actions. My getting out of bed when the alarm goes off fits into a sequence of actions all performed with the intention of arriving at work on time, all directed towards that end. That sequence in turn fits into a much larger pattern of many actions all performed with the intention of doing my job efficiently. My concern to do my job efficiently can be seen as part of an overall pattern of my life in which I have certain aims and certain priorities. Doing my job efficiently is just one of these. I may be aware of this pattern and consciously strive to follow it or it may be that the pattern can be inferred by an observer but I am not myself fully aware of the plan I appear to be pursuing.

Seeking intentional patterns in individual works of art is like seeking patterns in one small sequence of actions. If we turn now to other ways in which we infer an artist's intentions and use that inference in interpreting his or her works, we can see that we are fitting the individual work into a larger pattern, just as we fit individual actions, or small sequences of actions, into a larger pattern. If we bring in evidence from other work by the same artist, we are assuming that a coherent pattern will be formed not just by, say, *The Tempest* on its own but by all Shakespeare's late plays. Consider again one of the sentences from Traversi's discussion of Shakespeare's last plays quoted at the beginning of this chapter: 'That these comedies . . . form a close artistic unity is revealed clearly in the pattern discernible in their respective plots.'[9] Similarly, if we bring in evidence from an author's unpublished manuscripts we do so because that evidence fits together with the published work into a coherent pattern. Critics often also refer to works read by the artist, as Kathleen Raine does in her discussion of Blake. This is evidence of a rather different kind in that it does not come from work created by the artist. We are still, however, assuming that we can trace a link between what the artist read and what he produced himself. We do not look for such a relationship by enquiring into inaccessible processes in the artist's mind. We look for parallels between what he or she read and what he or she produced. There would be no point in quoting Hermetic texts to illuminate Blake if there were no evidence that Blake had read these texts and no apparent echoes of them in his works.

If we were strictly to maintain that only evidence from the text of the work under discussion is admissible in criticism, we would in effect be saying that we should look only for small-scale patterns in art. Patterns within individual works would be all right but patterns formed by a whole series of works, or by a series of works together with other material, would not be permitted. There is no good reason to say this. Indeed, our appreciation of works of art can often be enhanced by seeing those works in a broader context. Traversi's discussion of *The Tempest* is made more illuminating by his parallels from other late plays of Shakespeare. Blake's 'The Tyger' is hard to make sense of on its own and the differing interpretations offered by Raine and Hirsch both seek to help us understand the poem by placing it in a wider framework.

Large-scale artistic patterns may be constructed not only by putting together works by the same author but also by putting together works which use the same forms and conventions. Earlier in this chapter I argued that placing a work in relation to other works which use the same forms and conventions is one way of relating it to the original audience's expectations. At the same time it also relates it to the artist's intentions. An artist very often works within a particular tradition, deliberately producing a work in a certain genre. For example, Virgil in composing the *Aeneid* was trying to write a poem in the same genre as Homer's *Iliad* and *Odyssey* while Milton in composing *Paradise Lost* was trying in his turn to emulate Virgil and Homer. The evidence that Virgil was trying to write in the same genre as Homer does not lie in any statements of intention by Virgil distinct from the poem itself, for none such survive. It lies in the many close parallels between passages of the *Aeneid* and passages of the two Homeric poems.[10] Some lines by Propertius indicate clearly that Virgil's own contemporaries took him to be emulating Homer:

> cedite Romani scriptores, cedite Grai!
> nescio quid maius nascitur Iliade.

(Give way, Roman writers, give way, Greek writers. Something greater than the *Iliad* is being born.)[11]

The pattern of connections between Virgil and Homer is worth making because it enhances our appreciation of Virgil's poetry.

The patterns of coherence which can be found among works by one artist, between an artist's works and his or her reading, or between the work of one artist and the work of another using the same genre need not all be consciously produced. Suppose that we travelled back in time to the first century BC and discussed with Virgil the many reminiscences of Homer in his *Aeneid*. It is quite possible that some of the reminiscences found by careful scholars would be a surprise to him and would not have been put into the poem deliberately. Not all artistic creation is the result of careful conscious planning. We are influenced by what we have read and seen and heard without necessarily being aware of it. It seems to me, nevertheless, quite legitimate to describe all the

Homeric parallels in the *Aeneid* as intentional. Some may be the
product of what is often paradoxically called 'unconscious intention'. Such a phenomenon must be allowed, in action and in
language as well as in art, if we are to say that intentional actions,
language, and art are those in which patterns may be discerned by
others. My leaving the breakfast dishes unwashed is not unintentional just because I had not previously planned to do so. If I am
questioned about this action I am likely to recognize it as intentional. I may also not be aware of the way in which my arriving at
work on time fits into the pattern of my life as a whole but when
the relationship is pointed out to me I am likely to acknowledge
it. Virgil would, I think, have recognized all his Homeric reminiscences well enough when they were drawn to his attention even if
he did not consciously plan them all. Shakespeare may or may
not have planned the connections of plot and theme which
Traversi finds among his last plays but I doubt if he would have
denied their presence once they were pointed out to him.[12]

I have been arguing that patterns of coherence among works by
the same artist, between works by one artist and other material
such as that artist's reading, and among works in the same genre
may all be evidence of the artist's intention, including 'unconscious intention', and that all are admissible in criticism. But
suppose I find a pattern by putting together a Chinese poem, a
West African tribal song, and Dante's *Inferno* and this pattern
leads me to a new and exciting interpretation of Dante. I am not
claiming that Dante knew the Chinese poem or the West African
song, I just think the results of putting all three together are
exciting. It is conceivable that there might be some common
feature of the human condition which all three express and that
the juxtaposition of the Chinese poem and the West African song
helps us to perceive that feature in Dante more clearly. Unless this
is the case it is hard to see how our understanding of the *Inferno*
can genuinely be advanced by a pattern which takes no account of
Dante's knowledge and interests, nor of the time and place in
which he lived, nor of the audience he wrote for. We cannot find
just any old pattern in a work of art. Normally the pattern must
bear some relation to the author and the point of origin if we are
to produce a justifiable interpretation.

So far I have (quite deliberately) said very little about artists'
explicit statements of their intentions, although I have mentioned

an artist's recognition of patterns produced without conscious planning. Artists' statements of intentions are often not available. Only for artists of the relatively recent past do documents survive such as letters and diaries in which the planning of their work is described while only living artists can give interviews and be asked what their intentions were. Even where such statements are available they are often unreliable. We are not always the best interpreters of our own actions and artists are not always the best interpreters of their own works. What is more, artists often dislike being quizzed about their own works and they may well offer insincere and misleading answers. Before the work is produced an artist can only tell us about his or her conscious intentions. The work may well turn out not to be in accordance with these, for intentions may change as the work proceeds and elements may creep in which, though not consciously intended, can subsequently be seen to cohere in the total pattern. Where we have access to an artist's progressive revisions of a work we may be able to see how the pattern is modified as the work is polished. Revision may be evidence of an attempt to bring the work into harmony with a pre-existing intention but unless we know that the artist specified his intentions in great detail in advance, revision is better seen as evidence of the way intentions develop and are modified as the pattern which exhibits them is brought into being. Leishman's discussion of Milton's 'Lycidas', used as an example at the beginning of this chapter, makes extensive use of Milton's revisions of the text in just this way.

More important than what artists consciously have in mind before they begin is whether, if they are available to be asked, they can subsequently recognize the patterns we find in their work. Beardsley discusses A. E. Housman's poem '1887', written on the occasion of Queen Victoria's Golden Jubilee.[13] The concluding lines,

> Get you the sons your fathers got,
> And God will save the Queen.

were assumed by Frank Harris to be sarcastic but Housman indignantly denied that he had intended anything other than sincere patriotism. Beardsley, ignoring any distinction between sarcasm and irony, takes the view that if competent critics found irony in the poem, then 'we should conclude that it is ironical, no matter what Housman says'. This seems to me to be wrong. The poem may be accidentally ironical but it cannot be unqualifiedly ironical if Housman's denial was sincere. The lines, on the face of it, are ambiguous: they can be taken as straightforward Victorian patriotism or as sneering irony. Housman's denial of irony dissolves the ambiguity. There is a temptation to read the lines as ironical because read as straightforward patriotism they make an unimpressive ending to a not very good poem. It would be so much cleverer, we think, if they were not straightforward. But since we cannot foist Harris's cleverness upon Housman we are not justified in regarding the lines as ironical.

If we reflect on critical practice we shall find that artists' explicit statements of intention are usually appealed to either as support for an interpretation already developed on the basis of the text or in cases where the text is so puzzling that we do not know what to make of it. It will help here to return to the parallel between intention in art and intention in language. Normally we treat what somebody says as self-explanatory. We do not look beyond what has been said when we enquire what meaning was intended. The cases where we do ask the speaker what he or she meant are cases where we cannot understand the words otherwise. Similarly, we only ask the artist what he meant when he has not succeeded in making his intention plain in his work. Just as we normally intend our linguistic utterances to be understood on their own, without further explanation on our part, so the artist intends his work to be understood without further explanation by him.[14]

The artist produces his or her work to be understood by an audience. At this point the audience's expectations re-enter the picture. An artist will use the forms and conventions of his or her own day, following the moral, social, and political assumptions of the time, not only because this is what he or she knows, but because this is what the audience know. Of course artists can choose to use a style and a set of assumptions which most of their audience will regard as old-fashioned and artists may puzzle audiences because they are innovating either artistically or in their moral, social, and political attitudes. Yet there must be some point of contact with the audience's expectations or else the audience will be not just puzzled but bored and indifferent. There must be some thread the audience can pick up in order to trace a way through the labyrinth of the work presented to them.

From the point of view of the critic removed from the original place or time of the work's production the audience's expectations are not only of theoretical importance. They are also practically useful since it will often be easier to find out about them than about the artist's intentions. We have no record of Aeschylus' intentions in writing the *Oresteia* but we can discover quite a lot about the society and the culture he was writing in and what we discover helps us to determine which of the patterns we find in the *Oresteia* offer the basis for a justifiable interpretation and which are anachronistic impositions, mere creations of our own twentieth-century minds.

I have been arguing in this chapter that ultimately critical interpretation of a work of art cannot be justified by appeal to the text alone. Support must be sought from two sources, such evidence as is available for the artist's intentions and such evidence as is available for the expectations of the original audience. In practice these two types of evidence will often overlap. They also overlap in theory since artists normally produce their works with the expectations of an audience in mind.[15] Clearly there will be many cases where we cannot discover for certain which of several possible interpretations is correct because we do not have enough evidence about artist's intentions or audience's expectations. We will be able to rule out some wrong interpretations on the grounds that they neglect evidence of the types I have discussed but we will not be able to find one right interpretation. Is this purely a practical difficulty and is there at least a theoretical ideal of one and only one correct interpretation of a work?

E. D. Hirsch argued that in theory there is for every work one correct interpretation, which is the one the author intended.[16] In Hirsch's view to allow anything else would be to open up the field of criticism entirely and to be left with no standards by which to discriminate between interpretations. I argued in Chapter 6 that it was a mistake to try to understand the procedure of critics in terms of deductive argument from agreed premises to a proven conclusion. Hirsch too recognizes that criticism cannot attain the certainty of deductive proof. In his view the critic follows a logic of probability and his aim is to achieve a consensus that a particular interpretation is the most probable. Hirsch makes a distinction between the meaning of a literary work and its significance. Meaning is what the author intended to convey. The meaning of a text does not change and to discover this meaning is the task of interpretation. Significance, on the other hand, is what the audience finds in a work. Different audiences relate to a given work in different ways and Hirsch is happy to concede that a work's significance may change. We do not respond to the *Oresteia* in the way that the ancient Greeks did but, Hirsch holds, the meaning Aeschylus intended to convey remains the same.

Hirsch is concerned only with literary works and assumes a close analogy between 'meaning' as applied to literature and 'meaning' as applied to language. This analogy in fact presents problems as we shall see in the next chapter. Hirsch uses his distinction between meaning and significance to argue that in the end conformity with the artist's intentions is the sole criterion of valid interpretation. For Hirsch the original audience has no privileged status. Their expectations of the work and their response to it belong to the realm of significance. My view is not the same as Hirsch's: I have argued that interpretations may be justified in either or both of two ways, appeal to the artist's intentions and appeal to the expectations of the original audience. For some works one interpretation will emerge as the only justifiable one but for many works even if we had sufficient evidence to provide us with a thorough knowledge of both intentions and expectations there would still remain several justifiable interpretations. These might conflict with one another, for some works of art, some of the most interesting ones, just are radically ambiguous. Such ambiguity might itself be intended by the artist so that the Hirschian 'meaning' of the text is itself a set of alternatives.[17] However, ambiguity might also result from a conflict between artist's intentions and audience's expectations. In such a case Hirsch would say that the interpretation which conforms with the artist's intentions must be the correct one. It is not necessary to be so restrictive. To admit that a work of art can have more than one justifiable interpretation is not to say that 'anything goes', that there are no standards for criticism after all; it is to do justice to the richness and complexity of art.

As in the previous chapter I have concentrated here on works of literature and my examples have been largely drawn from literature. The artist's intentions and the audience's expectations are criteria of justifiable interpretation not only in literature but in all the arts. An interpretation of a painting is justified by consideration not only of the details of the painting itself but by reference to other works of the same artist and other works which use the same artistic conventions and by reference to the attitudes and assumptions of the artist and those for whom it was originally painted. Similarly, an interpretation of a piece of music is justified not only by consideration of the details of that piece but by reference to other works of the same composer and other pieces which use the same musical forms and by reference to the assumptions and attitudes of the composer and the audience for whom the piece was originally intended. There may be more than one justifiable interpretation of a painting or a piece of music, just as there may be more than one justifiable interpretation of a work of literature. To demand that a critic prove his or her interpretation of a work to be the only correct one is to demand the impossible. To demand that a critic, to be taken seriously, justify his or her interpretation in accordance with the procedure and the standards outlined in this and the previous chapter is to recognize that criticism is not a game but a discipline which, properly practised, can enhance our appreciation of works of art.

8

Meaning and truth

We have seen that E. D. Hirsch holds that the task of interpretation is to discover the meaning of a work of literature. This claim sounds uncontroversial since critics quite often describe works of art as having meaning. Sometimes too they declare that a work conveys or expresses truth. A critic of Greek tragedy, Oliver Taplin, writing about Aeschylus, says he is concerned to elucidate 'the meaning of a tragedy' but insists that this is not something conveyed by the words alone. His concern is with 'dramatic meaning' and 'visual meaning'.[1] A philosopher, Jonathan Barnes, can speak of 'the elementary truth that works of art very often do purvey truths . . .'.[2] While such talk in terms of meaning and truth may be applied to music and to visual art as well as drama, it is most often applied to literature. Typical examples are John Bayley's mention, when writing about Henry James's *The Golden Bowl*, of 'the perennial controversy about the novel's intention and meaning', and Angus Calder's claim that in *Old Mortality*, 'Scott strikes out to reach the human truth'.[3]

The fact that the medium of literature is language explains why the terms 'meaning' and 'truth' are so readily applied to literature. Statements in language have meaning and are true or false and it is an easy slide to speak of the meaning and the truth or falsity of works composed of such statements. The concepts of meaning and truth as applied to language are much studied in both philosophy and linguistics and are by no means free from difficulty. Nevertheless, in everyday usage when we speak of statements in language as true or meaningful, we are using familiar and on the whole comprehensible notions. There are criteria for the truth or falsity of statements and rules of logic which govern the relations between true and false statements, notably a rule that the contradiction of a true statement must be false. Meaning is less straightforward but we regularly assume that there is a clear distinction between a meaningful statement and a meaningless one, that we can explain the meaning of a statement to a child or a foreigner who has not understood, and that a statement with more than one meaning is ambiguous. It is much less clear what is meant by talk of the meaning or truth of a work of art.

Suppose one critic says that Henry James's short story, *The Turn of the Screw*, a story about a governess and two small children who seem to be possessed by evil ghosts, has a Freudian meaning and is really about the sexual repression of the governess, while another says it is to be understood as a comment on nineteenth-century English attitudes to children; a third may say it is simply a gripping ghost-story with no further meaning at all. For E. D. Hirsch the only possible meaning of the story would be the meaning James intended. According to my own argument in Chapter 7, the story could be ambiguous, it could have more than one meaning, but a justifiable interpretation of it must be supported not only by evidence drawn from the text but also by evidence of James's intentions and of his original audience's expectations. (Evidence of intention, we must remember, does not just mean explicit statements of intention. It includes evidence drawn from other works by the same person and the other kinds of evidence mentioned on p. 99.) It is unlikely that either James or his original readers would have known of Freud's psychoanalytic theories which were only just being formulated when *The Turn of the Screw* was written. Nevertheless, an original reader might have wondered, as the modern reader wonders, whether there is not something rather peculiar about the governess. In her narrative she makes comments such as, 'I used to wonder how my little charges could help guessing that I thought strange things about them; and the circumstance that these things only made them more interesting was not by itself a direct aid to keeping them in the dark.' At the start of her final confrontation with the little boy, Miles, she says, 'We continued silent while the maid was with us—as silent, it whimsically occurred to me, as some young couple who, on their wedding-journey, at the inn, feel shy in the presence of the waiter.'[4] I shall return later to the question whether a Freudian or quasi-Freudian interpretation of the story can be justified. For the moment my concern is to elucidate what is meant by saying that this or any other interpretation of *The Turn of the Screw* tells us the 'meaning' of the story.

A similar problem arises in the case of truth: the Freudian critic will say *The Turn of the Screw* expresses truths about unconscious human drives, the second critic that it expresses truths about Victorian England, the third critic that the question of truth does not arise here. Do these three critics all mean the same thing by 'truth'? Are there criteria for determining when a work expresses truth? Can only meaningful works express truth, just as only meaningful statements can be true or false, and do all works that do not express truth express falsehood?

Since the terms 'meaning' and 'truth' apply most readily and most comprehensibly to language, it is natural to suppose that their application to language is the paradigm from which other applications are derived and that when we apply these concepts to literature or any other art we are treating that art as a language. We have already seen that the role of intention in art can be illuminated by considering intention in relation to both language and action. We might, therefore, hope that talk of meaning and truth in art and literature could similarly be elucidated by an analogy between art and language.

Some caution is required here, however. Just because linguistic meaning is the most striking and most discussed type of meaning, we should not forget that the term 'meaning' can be used in a variety of ways. There are plenty of other kinds of meaning beside linguistic meaning: spots can mean measles, a nod can mean agreement and a red light can mean 'Stop!' It is worth noticing that the other kinds of meaning I have listed are either natural symptoms (the spots) or signs whose meaning is determined by convention. (A nod only means agreement in some cultures, while in others it means the opposite; the meaning of traffic-lights is laid down explicitly in the Highway Code.) Even when considering language we need to distinguish between what the speaker means by what he says and the meaning of the sentences he utters. Thus 'You're standing on my foot' is not usually just a statement of fact; the speaker usually means by it 'Please get off my foot', but that is not what he says. One can imagine an amusing dialogue with a Martian who failed to realize this: 'Oh, I'm standing on your foot, am I? How interesting!' 'But I meant you to get off my foot.' 'Oh I see! Why didn't you say so?' Such a scenario brings out clearly that here too implicit conventions of a cultural kind are involved. In general, meaning always involves rules for correlating what has meaning with what is meant, the signifier with the signified. These rules may be natural, as in the case of the spots which mean measles, but are more often conventional. The rules may vary enormously in explicitness and precision. The meaning of statements in language is governed by rules which are relatively explicit and precise but very complex. We should not forget the possibility that the meaning of works of art might be more like other types of meaning.

'Truth' is much more restricted in its application than meaning. Spots, nods, and roadsigns cannot be true or false, nor can orders, warnings, requests, wishes, or questions, whether expressed in language or by other means. Only assertions can properly be true or false. Here too the analogy between art and language needs careful handling. We usually say that works of art convey or express or even reveal truth rather than that they are true, and this suggests that artistic truth and linguistic truth may not be of the same kind. (When critics speak of artistic truth, they are sometimes concerned with whether the artist is giving expression to something he truly feels, that is, with sincerity. Artistic truth in this sense bears no relation to linguistic truth as can be seen if we reflect that it is one thing to ask whether a statement is true and another to ask whether the speaker made it sincerely, believing it to be true. I am not here concerned with this concept, better described as sincerity than as truth, and shall say no more about it.)

With these caveats in mind, let us explore ways in which meaning and truth in language might cast light on meaning and truth in art. I have already said that meaning requires rules, however vague, however inexplicit, for correlating what has meaning with what is meant. This is the aspect of language that linguists are referring to when they talk about semantics and semantic rules. But a language, as distinct from just any system with meaning, also requires rules for combining the elements within it, a syntax. It is the rules of syntax, not the rules of semantics, which determine that a sentence composed entirely of pronouns is not a meaningful English sentence or that 'The dog bit the man' means something different from 'The man bit the dog'. Both syntax and semantics have a part to play in the interpretation of linguistic meaning and if meaning in art is really like meaning in language we should expect conventions which govern the internal combination of elements as well as conventions which correlate elements within the work with phenomena external to it. Oliver Taplin, in his account of the dramatic conventions of Greek tragedy, seems to be claiming exactly this. He describes his book on Aeschylus as 'a contribution towards a "grammar" of the dramatic technique of the Greek tragedians'.[5] By 'grammar' he means what I mean by 'syntax'. He wants to show, for example, that it is a convention in Greek tragedy for there to be an exit by an actor before a song by the chorus; departures from this convention, when not attributable to incompetence in the playwright or to error in the textual tradition, are deliberate and calculated for artistic effect in a similar way to that in which departures from regular syntax by a poet like Gerard Manley Hopkins are deliberate and calculated for artistic effect. Similarly, historians of Renaissance art claim not just that individual elements in a picture have iconographic significance and refer to particular concepts, but that there are conventions which govern the combination of such elements. Edgar Wind, for example, not only interprets the three Graces in Botticelli's *Primavera* (see Plate 4) as chastity, beauty, and pleasure respectively but draws further inferences from the calm and firm way in which the three figures are linked together and from the contrast between them and the less harmonious group of three on the other side of the picture.[6] If at least some art has something analogous to a syntax, as well as a system of semantics, the analogy with language begins to look more worth exploring.

One way of exploring this analogy would be to consider the truth-value of statements in works of fiction. Are the accounts of the doings of fictional persons like George Eliot's Dorothea or Flaubert's Madame Bovary, Virgil's Aeneas or Tennyson's Lady of Shalott, true or false? It seems odd to say they are true since they are statements about people who never existed, mentioning objects and perhaps places which do not exist either, and recounting events which never happened. To say they are false is to deny any distinction between statements made in fiction which are to be regarded as true within the fiction, such as the statement from *Middlemarch*, 'Dorothea went up to her room to answer Mr Casaubon's letter',[7] and ordinary false statements about real people or things, such as, 'George Eliot did not write a novel called *Middlemarch*'. To say they are meaningless is to leave us with no means of distinguishing them from actual nonsense.

One recurrently popular solution to this problem is to say that the writer of a work of fiction, in making such statements, is not asserting anything, is not making any claims which may be judged as true or false; the question of truth does not arise. Such statements might be true or false within the work concerned—it can be true or false that, in George Eliot's novel, *Middlemarch*, Dorothea went up to her room to answer Mr Casaubon's letter—but they are not, on this view, true or false about anything in the real world. However, consideration of such statements is not going to take us very far with the enquiry whether and how a whole work of literature can express truth. Works of literature are not entirely composed of statements referring to fictional persons, objects, places, or events, and some works of literature do not contain any such statements: many lyric poems do not, nor do other types of writing which can be regarded as literature such as essays, travel books, history, and biography. Moreover, the truths that works of literature are often thought to express are not truths about any particular persons but truths of a general kind about human nature or society or the way the world is. If *Middlemarch* tells us things which are true, what it tells us is about human behaviour and human societies in general, not about imaginary persons living in an imaginary place.

One might suppose that the truth of such statements within a particular work was relevant to its overall truth. Could a work of literature full of mutually contradictory statements tell us something true? It could very well be doing just that, telling us that the world is a contradictory and confusing place. Whether the statements in a work contradict one another certainly affects the overall coherence of the work, but is not relevant to its truth. It looks then as though the problem of the truth-value of statements about fictional persons, or objects, or places, or events, is not relevant to the question of the truth of literary works as a whole.

Another possible area for exploration, more illuminating for our purposes, is that of statements which use language in some figurative way. There has been a certain amount of philosophical discussion of such statements, concentrating on metaphor and concerned with how, and indeed whether, metaphors have meaning and whether there is such a thing as metaphorical truth. A good deal of light can be cast on our problem from both the insights and the deficiencies of such discussion. It is important first to get clear why the discussion of metaphor is relevant. It is *not* because literature uses a lot of metaphors. It does do so, and metaphors in literature tend to be more striking as well as more common than in ordinary speech. But metaphors are not confined to literature, nor are they necessary to it: a plain narrative or a simple descriptive passage may use no metaphors and may be all the more telling for that. The reason why a consideration of meaning and truth in relation to metaphor may cast light on meaning and truth in relation to literature is that problems arise in the same way in both cases.

Most of those who discuss metaphor assume that there is such a thing as metaphorical meaning and try to explain how this differs from and is related to literal meaning. A statement such as 'Life's but a walking shadow' is said to be literally false but metaphorically true. We can try to give a literal paraphrase of it such as, 'Life is something frail and insubstantial which does not last long', but such a paraphrase cannot say everything the metaphor does. However much we extend the paraphrase, trying to spell out all the implications of calling life 'a walking shadow', we cannot make explicit all that Shakespeare's phrase conjures up in the mind. Many philosophers recognize that there is something very odd about saying that 'Life's but a walking shadow' is metaphorically true, for what would it be for such a statement to be metaphorically false? What are the criteria for metaphorical truth and falsity supposed to be? If there is something odd about metaphorical truth, perhaps there is something odd about metaphorical meaning. Perhaps metaphors do not mean but only suggest or evoke or have associations. All these issues may be paralleled by issues arising in relation to works of literature. A number of the philosophers who discuss metaphor are quite aware of this but they stick to simple examples of metaphor of the type 'A is B' hoping to see the problems and their solution most clearly in simple cases. I propose to examine what bearing these discussions have on works of literature, thinking for the moment of such works as metaphors writ large, as though *Middlemarch*, for example, were an extended and complex metaphorical expression of a view about human beings and their relationships within society.

Theories of metaphor may be divided into three broad groups.[8] First come *comparison theories*, whose illustrious ancestor is the account of metaphor given by Aristotle. On a comparison theory, in saying 'Life's but a walking shadow' we are comparing life to a walking shadow, saying that it is like a walking shadow. The metaphorical statement means what the equivalent literal statement of comparison means and is true or false accordingly. What then does the comparison 'Life is like a walking shadow' mean? Only when we have discovered what the statement means will we be able to determine whether it is true or false. To explain the meaning we will have to specify the respects in which the two compared things are alike. One can begin upon this task, just as one can begin upon the task of paraphrasing a metaphor: both life and a shadow do not last long, both are frail and insubstantial. Here already we must pause. Life is not literally insubstantial as a shadow is. Perhaps rather life is *like* something insubstantial. But then we have another comparison to be unpacked. A further complication is the description of the shadow as 'walking'. We have here what is really a double metaphor, for shadows do not walk literally. Must we then say that life is like a walking figure who is like a shadow and try to specify all the respects in which life, walkers, and shadows are similar? A long and potentially infinite task seems to be before us. An attempt to apply the comparison theory to a genuine example of a rich and evocative metaphor shows up the weaknesses of the theory. Just as we cannot completely paraphrase a metaphor, so we cannot always specify literally respects in which the compared things are alike and it is often difficult or impossible to do so exhaustively.

Difficulties such as these about developing a comparison theory of metaphor satisfactorily have led to the second group of theories, *interaction theories*. Such a theory is particularly associated with the name of Max Black. On Black's theory the meanings of 'life' and 'walking shadow' in 'Life's but a walking shadow' interact, in such a way that neither term means quite what it did before. We think of life as a walking shadow. Black illustrates what it is to think of *A* as *B* by examples where we can see a geometrical figure in a number of different ways. Considerable imaginative effort may be required to see or think of a figure in an unfamiliar manner. Thus the Star of David figure may be seen either as two superimposed triangles or as a hexagon surrounded by six small triangles:

To see the figure in the two different ways we must concentrate on different perceptual aspects of it.[9] Similarly, in thinking of life as a walking shadow, we concentrate on certain aspects of life, walkers, and shadows to the exclusion of others; to think of life as a walking shadow and to think of it as a tale told by an idiot are to think of it in two different ways. Black is reluctant to speak of metaphorical statements as either true or false. A successful metaphor, he thinks, is more like a good map or diagram. It 'shows how things are'. There are some interesting suggestions here, which we shall be returning to, but Black's theory has its own difficulties. He has been criticized, and rightly so, for an inability to make clear what he means by 'interaction' and in what sense 'life' and 'walking shadow' are supposed to 'change their meaning'. They are not supposed to lose the meanings they had before in such a change, and the change lasts only as long as the metaphor, with no effect on the use of the terms in other contexts. This is a change in meaning unlike any other and not readily comprehensible.

Dissatisfaction with both comparison and interaction theories has led to the development of a third type of theory, using the notion of a *speech act*. This notion was originally introduced into philosophy by J. L. Austin to explain what is going on when we say, 'I promise to meet you at 7 p.m.' or, 'I am sorry I stood on your foot'. These are not statements about any state of affairs but are themselves the performance of a special kind of action: to perform the act of promising is to say 'I promise that . . .'; to perform the act of apologizing is to say 'I am sorry that . . .'. Such actions as these, performed by means of speech, are speech acts.

A crude speech act theory of metaphor would hold that in saying 'Life's but a walking shadow', I am not making any statement about a state of affairs but am performing an act of metaphorizing, or some such. Just to say this, however, will not help us much unless the theory explains what it is to perform such an act. A more complex and sophisticated speech act theory of metaphor has been put forward by John Searle. Searle regards metaphor as an indirect speech act, that is, a speech act where what the speaker *means by* what he says is different from the meaning of the sentences he utters. Searle's paradigm of an indirect speech act is a case of the kind mentioned earlier where I say, 'You're standing on my foot' but what I mean by this is, 'Please get off my foot'; that is, 'You're standing on my foot' is an indirect speech act of requesting you to move. Metaphor, Searle suggests, is a special, complex case of an indirect speech act, a special case of saying one thing and meaning something else. On this view when I say, 'Life's but a walking shadow', I am saying something which is literally false; what I mean by what I say, however, is that life is frail and insubstantial, and does not last long. Searle thinks there is a complex set of principles according to which metaphors are produced and understood and attempts to set out those principles.

Searle's view differs from both comparison and interaction theories in holding that metaphorical meaning is meaning of a different kind from literal meaning. A metaphorical statement is not equivalent to a literal statement of comparison; nor does it involve a change of some inexplicable kind in the meaning of the words used; its meaning lies in what the speaker means by it. On this view metaphorical statements could not be true or false in themselves any more than requests or apologies or promises could be, although the statements which paraphrase a metaphor ('life is frail, insubstantial, and does not last long') may be true or false. It is because making a metaphorical statement is a different kind of speech act from making a literal statement that there seems to be more in a metaphor than in any paraphrase of it. If I say, 'Life's but a walking shadow', I am conveying the idea that life is frail, insubstantial, and does not last long by a different means from those I would be using if I simply made a literal statement about life. This view too is not without its difficulties. The most telling objection is that if metaphor were some kind of speech act the figurative character of metaphorical statements would disappear when such statements are transformed into indirect speech. 'Tom said that he was sorry' reports a speech act but is not itself the act of apologizing as 'I am sorry' is. But 'Shakespeare said that life's but a walking shadow' still contains a metaphor; it is not just a report of a metaphor.[10]

None of the existing theories of metaphor is fully satisfactory, though all contain insights of some interest. All of them admit that a relation of similarity between the subject of the metaphor and the predicate metaphorically attributed to it is involved but they disagree over whether the similarity is actually stated in the metaphor (the view of comparison theories) or whether seeing such a similarity is part of how we understand the metaphor (the view of both interaction and speech act theories). Max Black, in trying to elucidate how we can produce and understand metaphors by perceiving relevant similarities, introduces the notion of 'thinking as' and illustrates it with examples of 'seeing as'. My survey of theories of metaphor also shows up a number of points of dispute and unanswered questions. There is dispute over whether metaphorical statements can be said to be true: they can be on a comparison view but on both interaction and speech act views they could only be true in some special sense. Black suggests that a successful metaphor 'shows how things are' rather than being true. The way in which metaphors mean is unclear and the interaction theory in particular invokes a special and somewhat mysterious notion of change of meaning. This may raise doubts about whether the concept of meaning is really applicable here at all. Linked to this is the question whether metaphors can be paraphrased: if they cannot there is something very odd about their 'meaning', for statements with meaning of a regular kind can be paraphrased and translated according to semantic and syntactic rules. Searle attempts to explain why we feel that metaphors cannot be paraphrased and to offer rules for their production and understanding but his attempt is not completely successful. As for unanswered questions the most notable one which all the philosophers evade is why we use metaphor so much, whence comes its power and its effectiveness.

The insights that arise from these theories of metaphor can all be applied in one way or another to the larger case of literature. To take first the role of similarity: if *The Turn of the Screw* really does have a Freudian meaning there must be some similarities between the surface of the story and the workings of the unconscious mind as understood in Freudian terms. This may sound strange and the notion of similarity does need to be extended here. When Edmund Wilson developed a Freudian interpretation of *The Turn of the Screw*,[11] he did not simply draw attention to passages of the kind I quoted at the beginning of this chapter. He claimed to discover not so much similarities as correspondences between elements in the text and Freudian symbols. The fact that the male ghost in the story first appears on a tower corresponds to the Freudian role of phallic symbols such as towers, while the water of the lake beside which the female ghost appears is taken to be connected with female sexuality and motherhood because water in Freudian theory is a symbol for birth. In the case of *Middlemarch* George Eliot's own prelude to the novel begins with a paragraph about St Theresa of Avila whose 'passionate ideal nature demanded an epic life' and who 'found her epos in the reform of a religious order'. She goes on to suggest a correspondence between the saint and her heroine, Dorothea:

Many Theresas have been born who found for themselves no epic life wherein there was a constant unfolding of far-resonant action; perhaps only a life of mistakes . . . perhaps a tragic failure . . . these later-born Theresas were helped by no coherent social faith and order which could perform the function of knowledge for the ardently willing soul.

George Eliot here is inviting us to compare Dorothea's nature with St Theresa's and at the same time to contrast their opportunities for noble and heroic action. In the novel itself Dorothea is compared not only with St Theresa but also with the Greek tragic heroine Antigone.[12] To say that *Middlemarch* is about the limitations imposed by a society of a certain kind upon those with a capacity for 'an epic life' would be to give a possible interpretation of the novel, a possible account of its meaning, and one which seems indicated by the attention which the author herself draws to correspondences between her characters and those of earlier history and literature. The notion of correspondence invoked here is complex and I shall return to it. The complexity is no objection to regarding it as parallel to the notion of similarity in metaphor; that too is complex and gives theorists of metaphor a lot of trouble.

'Thinking as' or 'seeing as' also has its analogue in literary interpretation. We saw in Chapter 6 that an interpretation of a work of literature must be tested by seeing whether the text can be read in accordance with that interpretation. '*The Turn of the Screw* may be read as a Freudian fantasy' would be a perfectly natural account of the Edmund Wilson interpretation of that story and if we are to test Wilson's interpretation then what we must do is precisely to read the story as he would have us do and see if it all makes sense in those terms. Similarly, with *Middlemarch*: to read it as a story of general application we must look out for certain elements in it, pay attention to references to St Theresa or Greek tragedy, overlook some of the details of the setting, and so on. This is all analogous to thinking of life as a walking shadow, where we concentrate on certain aspects of life, walkers, and shadows, or to seeing a Star of David figure as two superimposed triangles.

We can also learn from the points of dispute and the unanswered questions which arise in relation to metaphor. Talk of truth is as problematic when applied to literature as when applied to metaphorical statements. To assimilate talk of literary works expressing truth to the use of 'true' in logic only produces obscurity and puzzlement. For truth in this sense we would expect criteria of truth which a work could satisfy and a clear notion of the contradiction that would result when a 'true' work was set against a 'false' one. We might also expect that the work claimed to be true should be an internally coherent set of true statements. Attempts to define truth in literature along these lines soon run into difficulties. Some progress may be made by applying to the large-scale case of literature Max Black's idea that a metaphor 'shows how things are'. We move firmly away from logical truth if we say that *The Turn of the Screw*, in expressing a truth about unconscious human drives, shows us how things are concerning such drives (if we accept Freudian theory) or that *Middlemarch*, in expressing truths about human behaviour and human societies, shows us how things are concerning such behaviour and such societies.

The language of 'showing how things are' requires further examination, however. Maps and diagrams too 'show how things are', they give an accurate presentation of some state of affairs. Literature and metaphors, like maps and diagrams, show rather than state, but what they show, if describable at all, is better described in terms of possibility than in terms of fact. More useful here than talk of 'showing how things are' would be talk of 'showing how things might be'. Suppose, for the sake of argument, that *The Turn of the Screw* can be read as a Freudian fantasy, that James, although probably ignorant of Freud, did intend to present the governess as thwarted and neurotic and that his original readers could have understood the story in this way. Even if I do not believe that sexual repression can really make anyone speak and behave quite as James's governess does, I could still accept that the story offers a compelling picture of what an extreme case of repression might be like, I could accept that the story shows how things might be, but deny that it shows how things really are. The analogy with metaphor would be to admit that 'Life's but a walking shadow' is an effective way of conveying the idea that life is frail, insubstantial, and does not last long but to deny that life is in fact any of those things.

There is much to be said for the view that metaphorical statements are successful or effective rather than true and for the parallel view that works of literature which present some general theory or view of the world do so successfully or effectively rather than truly. In considering literature we do not withhold our aesthetic appreciation from works which give an effective presentation of views we do not ourselves accept. One need not be a Roman Catholic to judge whether Evelyn Waugh succeeds in presenting a Catholic view of the world in *Brideshead Revisited*; whether the tenets of Catholicism are true and whether *Brideshead Revisited* is a successful novel are separate questions. Furthermore, what a work of literature shows may be too complex and many-sided to be describable as a distinct view, let alone a theory. A work may be successful and effective not only if it presents a theory which is not in fact true but also if it presents no theory or general view at all. For these reasons the language of truth is better not applied to literature, or to metaphor either.

We saw that the way in which metaphors have meaning is unclear, that it has been doubted whether the concept of meaning is really applicable here, and that these problems are related to the question whether metaphors can be paraphrased. Parallel difficulties arise in the case of literature. In what sense does *The Turn of the Screw* have a Freudian meaning, a meaning not perceived by all readers of the story? Some readers will strongly deny that such a story has any further meaning beyond what appears on the surface. I have toyed with the idea that James himself intended to present the governess as thwarted and neurotic. In fact the evidence for James's intentions is unclear. In the original version of his paper Edmund Wilson noted that James's own preface to the story alluded to the possibility that the governess's 'explanation' was not 'crystalline'. He also pointed out that in the collected edition of his work James included *The Turn of the Screw* not with his other ghost stories but with stories of another kind and he drew attention to the fact that the theme of the thwarted Anglo-Saxon spinster occurs elsewhere in James, in *The Bostonians*, for example. However, James's preface also describes the story as 'a fairy-tale' and 'a piece of ingenuity pure and simple'. In a later postscript to his essay Wilson admitted that James's notebooks make it plain that his conscious intention was to write a bona fide ghost story. He therefore fell back on a discussion of James's unconscious intentions as inferred from some of his other works and from events in his life at the time he wrote this particular story. Wilson's essay was first published in 1938 but the suggestion that readers might question the governess's sanity was already made by an anonymous reviewer in *The Critic* shortly after the story appeared in book form.[13] A Freudian, or at least a quasi-Freudian, reading of *The Turn of the Screw* does appear justifiable by the criteria I argued for in Chapter 7. Yet, quite apart from any uncertainty over James's intentions, there remains a strong objection to saying that this reading presents us with *the* meaning of the story. This is that it diminishes the tale: it does not account for all the elements in the text, it reduces a rich fabric to a simple theoretical scheme. A Freudian interpretation is just one among several justifiable interpretations of *The Turn of the Screw*. Similarly, despite the clear indications that George Eliot had the 'St Theresa' theme in mind, *Middlemarch* is not only about the limitations imposed by society upon a certain type of person. That is certainly an important aspect of the novel but there is much else in it besides. These points recall the objections raised by those who feel that metaphors always lose by being paraphrased, that there is more to 'Life's but a walking shadow' than the statement that life is something frail and insubstantial which does not last long.

Finally, the large unanswered question concerning metaphor is quite as large for literature. Why do we enjoy it; whence comes its power and effectiveness? The answer to this question is at least partly connected with the capacity of literature to point beyond itself, to mean, or show, or maybe just suggest, more than it states on the surface. The power of metaphor derives from comparable qualities. The unsolved problem is how to state the nature of these qualities and the role they play in our appreciation of both literature and metaphor.

The analogy between literature and metaphor may be further exploited if we turn to a type of literary criticism which does indeed treat literature in the way I have been proposing, as metaphor writ large. What I have in mind is the allegorical interpretation of literature. This method, much in vogue in late antiquity and the Middle Ages, might appear to be quite out of fashion in modern times. One might suppose that it had perished with the waning of explicitly allegorical literature and the rise of the Romantic movement. This would be a mistaken view. In practice allegorical interpretation is not dead, any more than allegorical literature is. It is only less dominant and less explicit about its procedures than it once was. Freudian interpretation of literature is a clear example of allegorical interpretation; what is Edmund Wilson's interpretation of *The Turn of the Screw* but a treatment of it as a Freudian allegory? Much the same is true of other types of interpretation which seek to interpret literature in terms of a preconceived theory: Marxist interpretation would be another example.[14] Despite the fact that it is still with us, allegory both in interpretation and in literature is frequently regarded as a hopeless and absurd proceeding. Explicit allegorical interpretation of works not known to have been written as allegorical is laughed out of court; no doubt this is why modern types of criticism which are in fact allegorical do not declare themselves to be so. The interesting question, though, is what is wrong with allegory? What is it doing that leads to its abrupt dismissal?

Deliberate allegory is often defined as extended metaphor and allegorical interpretation is interpretation which treats literature as just that. More specifically, it treats literature as metaphor capable of paraphrase, as a system of meaning which can be systematically decoded, as a language which can be translated. Thus in *The Turn of the Screw* Edmund Wilson takes it that particular objects in the story, the tower and the water, stand for or correspond to the phenomena which such objects stand for in Freudian psychoanalysis, that is, he assumes that there are clear semantic relations between elements in the story and phenomena outside the story. He also takes it that the relations between elements in the story are significant: the male ghost appears on the tower, the female ghost beside the lake. There is an analogy here with the syntactic relations which govern the combination of elements in a language. Such interpretation gives precision to the correspondences we noted earlier. In the case of metaphor, the exact respects in which life is like a walking shadow are hard to specify; with literary interpretation of a non-allegorical kind just how closely Dorothea in *Middlemarch* corresponds to St Theresa or to Antigone is also hard to specify and it would be hard to find similar correspondences for all the characters in *Middlemarch*. With allegorical interpretation these difficulties disappear. The theory or doctrine in terms of which the work is being interpreted provides an exact system of correspondences. Similarly, allegorical interpretation gives a straightforward sense to the notion of literature expressing truth. The theory or doctrine in terms of which the work is being interpreted tells us precisely what the truth in question is supposed to be and the work may be assessed for its accuracy in presenting that theory or doctrine.

Allegorical interpretation is of course quite admissible for deliberately allegorical literature. If we interpret Spenser's *The Faerie Queene* or Bunyan's *The Pilgrim's Progress* as allegory, we are doing what their authors intended us to do. These works were deliberately constructed as systems of meaning of the kind described and the allegorical interpretation is what their authors meant by them. The word 'allegory' means 'saying something else', that is, saying one thing and meaning something else. This is exactly how Searle describes what is going on in an indirect speech act and works of allegorical literature are indirect in just this kind of way. However, even a work intended as an allegory and understood as such by its original readers still contains more than the allegorical 'translation' of it. *The Pilgrim's Progress* is a gripping story, not a sermon. *The Faerie Queene* is a powerful and exciting poem, not a moral and political tract.

This brings us to the deficiencies of allegorical interpretation. Why does it fail to capture everything about even deliberately allegorical works, or, to put this another way, why did Spenser and Bunyan cast their ideas in fictional and literary form rather than writing theoretical treatises or abstract sermons? And why does allegorical interpretation seem radically deficient for works not intended to be read allegorically? The first question might be answered by the claim that, for deliberately allegorical works, the allegorical interpretation captures all the meaning; the rest is ornament. This would be an oversimplification, however. The meaning and the way it is conveyed cannot be so sharply separated. Something which is more than merely ornamental is lost if we set out only the theoretical plan of a deliberately allegorical work. This is even more clearly true when we turn to works that are not deliberately allegorical. The Freudian reading of *The Turn of the Screw* does work pretty well, and yet it loses something. As I said earlier, the story is diminished by such a reading. It seems to contain more, and a more that is not merely ornamental, than can be held in any such theoretical strait-jacket.

We are here at the very heart of the problem about literature and meaning. One of the things that makes literature worthwhile is that it points beyond itself, means more than it says on the surface. Yet this seems a kind of meaning which cannot readily be paraphrased or translated. An account of the meaning of, say, *Middlemarch* in terms of the restrictions which Victorian society placed upon people with a capacity for 'an epic life' leaves out much of the variety and individuality of the characters and the society portrayed in the book. Dorothea and the other central character, Lydgate, and the society in which they live are vivid and well-rounded and have individual traits; they are not just types which illustrate a preconceived thesis. The objection to allegorical interpretation is that it tries to pin the meaning down too much. Those who think deliberately allegorical literature is worthless see it simply as a system to be decoded and ignore the fact that the way the meaning is expressed is important. The notions of truth and falsity are not readily applicable at all to this kind of meaning that resists paraphrase, for if we cannot pin down what a work means, we cannot judge either whether what it means is true or whether that meaning is accurately presented.

The discussion so far has brought clarification of the problem rather than any solution. It has, I hope, become clearer what are the peculiarities of talk about meaning and truth in relation to literature but we seem as far as ever from any explanation of how such talk is to be understood. One radical solution would be to say that what the discussion has made clear is the inappropriateness of all such talk. 'Meaning' should be reserved for cases where there are rules for correlating signifier and signified, where paraphrase and translation are possible, and 'truth' should be similarly reserved for cases where the logical criteria for the application of 'true' and 'false' can be intelligibly applied. We should talk of literature suggesting or evoking ideas, of showing how things might be, of presenting a view, not of having meaning or expressing truth.

In the case of truth I have argued that talk of showing how things might be and of presenting a view is indeed more appropriate and that, when considering literature aesthetically, we are concerned with success and effectiveness in presentation rather than with truth, with the way in which showing is done rather than with what is shown. Should talk of meaning also be banished from literary criticism? If we substitute talk of suggesting or evoking ideas, we shall still want to ask just how a given work of literature suggests or evokes and to start looking at the way the story is presented, just as if we talk of meaning we shall have to look at the way the meaning is conveyed. There are two objections which might be made to this view. One is that the talk of suggesting and evoking will not be strong enough for all types of literature. To take the safe case of deliberately allegorical literature, it would be absurd to say that *The Pilgrim's Progress* only suggests the spiritual journey of the Christian soul. It does a good deal more than that. On the other hand, to say that *Middlemarch* suggests ideas about human behaviour in general is by no means absurd. Such vocabulary is more appropriate than talk of meaning in this case. Literature is very diverse and requires flexibility and diversity of criticism. What we are dealing with here is a continuum. At one end is literary meaning, at the other the delicate vocabulary of suggestion and evocation. Neither type of language on its own will interpret all literature for us. The second objection to the view that we should banish talk of meaning entirely is that such a view makes it sound as though meaning in other spheres is unproblematic. But it is far from being so. Meaning is one of the most intractable notions with which philosophers and linguists grapple. Let us not, then, banish any possible types of meaning until we understand more clearly how central cases of meaning work.

A second solution to our problem would be to appeal to all the other types of meaning I mentioned at the beginning of this chapter and have neglected since. Might not meaning in literature be more like the meaning of nods which signify agreement or red lights which mean 'Stop!' than like linguistic meaning after all?

In these types of meaning the rules are sometimes less clear and less precise than in language. If clear and precise rules cannot be applied to meaning in literature, perhaps the mistake lay in invoking the analogy of language at all. This suggestion will not take us very far. Meaning in literature is far more complex than the meaning of nods or traffic-lights and the complexity is something it shares with linguistic meaning. We can take from this suggestion the point that other types of meaning might help to shed light on literary meaning, just as they have sometimes been used by philosophers to shed light on linguistic meaning, but this is still a long way from a complete account of literary meaning.

A different analogy may help us here, though only by presenting more questions which have to be answered. Works of literature sometimes mean, sometimes only suggest; they show rather than state truth; the manner of the showing matters and is not easily detached from what is shown. All these points are also true of symbols, whether in art, literature, religion, or other spheres. Symbolism is often contrasted with allegory as being suggestive and indirect where allegory is explicit and all too direct. The distinction, if appropriate at all, is again a distinction between two ends of a continuum. If the figures in deliberately allegorical literature are more than just ciphers to be read off and dismissed, it is because they suggest more than their allegorical meaning, they function more like symbols. At the other end of the continuum are symbols which cannot be directly translated into any one set of meanings. The plague in Albert Camus's novel of that name would be an example. The plague can be understood in a number of different ways, as standing for the occupation of a city in wartime, for human mortality, and for evil and corruption in general and yet, recounted in horrifyingly realistic detail, it is more than all of them. If we were to take away the plague and substitute a different symbol, we should simply be destroying Camus's novel and writing a different one. The meaning of the plague and the manner in which it is described are indissolubly bound together. Does the plague mean or just suggest? Perhaps it comes somewhere between the two. Similar comments could be applied to non-literary symbols.

My examples in this chapter have been largely drawn from literary narratives of one kind or another but the points I have been making could be applied to literature in any mode or genre.

My suggestion that works of literature have meaning in a way analogous to that in which symbols have meaning, if correct, will be as true of lyric and drama as of narrative. To say this is not to solve our problem but is rather to suggest a new and difficult line of enquiry, into the meaning and function of symbols. Such an enquiry is outside the scope of this book. Recognition of the need for it reveals how problematic is the notion of meaning in literature. The critic's task is not to uncover one single meaning which a work must have; rather it is to present us with justifiable ways of reading the work and so help us to appreciate it.

9

Art and morals

We saw in Chapter 6 that critical interpretation and evaluation
are closely connected. Chapter 8 concluded that when considering literature aesthetically we are concerned with success and
effectiveness in presentation rather than with truth. 'Success' and
'effectiveness' are evaluative terms and the time has now come to
return from interpretation to evaluation. Often we admire works
of art for their formal qualities, for the coherent pattern of
relationships which they display.[1] Natural objects can be admired
in the same way. However, when we admire a work of art for its
success and effectiveness in presentation we are concerned not
only with its formal features but also with the view of the world or
the state of mind which it presents. We are concerned both with
the manner of showing and with what is shown and, as we saw in
Chapter 8, the two cannot be sharply separated. How then should
we judge the effective presentation of a morally corrupt view of
the world or an evil state of mind? Can we admire such a work as
aesthetically good and yet deplore it as morally bad?

The judgement that a work is morally bad usually carries with
it the claim that such a work will corrupt its audience. Claims
about the moral effects of works of art are not confined to representational art; even purely instrumental music and abstract
painting have sometimes been thought to improve or corrupt
those who hear or see them. However, such claims are more often
made about representational art and it is here that the problem
of the relationship between art and morals is at its most acute.
Within representational art debate has concentrated on arts which
represent human beings interacting with one another, that is, in
literature, including drama, and on films. In modern society the
possible effects of films on their audiences are of greater importance than the possible effects of literature or of plays. Many more
people see films, in cinemas, on television, and as videos, than
read books or go to the live theatre. Moreover, since films engage
both sight and hearing they can involve the spectator very fully

and for many people it is easier to be distracted from reading a book than from watching a film. (Plays likewise involve the spectator very fully. In this respect drama belongs with films rather than with literature which is read.) Despite the differences between books, plays, and films, the same issues about morality arise for them all. My discussion here, like the discussion in Chapters 6, 7, and 8, will concentrate on literature although I shall make some reference to films.

Arguments about morality and representational art often confuse moral questions about the content of art with moral questions about its effects. Any art which portrays human beings interacting with one another is bound to represent those human beings with character traits which are subject to moral assessment. The people represented may not be straightforwardly good or evil but they will display qualities such as kindness, generosity, or honesty, selfishness, meanness, or deceit. Some general view of the world in which we live may also be conveyed: for example, the world may be depicted as a place of gloom and horror in which wickedness flourishes while virtue goes unrewarded, or it may be depicted as a place in which good triumphs in the end and the wicked are justly punished. We should not too hastily assume a direct connection between moral content and moral effects. Evil characters in a novel might be represented in such a way as to make evil repellent to those who read the book. Similarly, the objection often made to violence in films is not simply that watching violence makes us violent. After all, watching violence and seeing its grim results might put us off altogether. Objection is taken to films which make violence attractive, films in which the doers of violent deeds are represented as glamorous and successful.

Some deny that art is of any moral relevance at all. While admitting that it can have moral content they declare that this content has no moral effect on the audience. Oscar Wilde, in the preface to *The Picture of Dorian Gray*, gave characteristically epigrammatic expression to this view:

There is no such thing as a moral or an immoral book. Books are well written or badly written. That is all. . . . The moral life of man forms part of the subject-matter of the artist, but the morality of art consists in the perfect use of an imperfect medium. No artist desires to prove anything . . . No artist has ethical sympathies.[2]

The opposite view holds that all art, whether representational or not, has moral effects on the audience. Those who maintain this position often regard the moral effects of art as a matter of political importance and therefore hold that art should be subject to state control. We shall see later that this was the view of Plato and that it is shared by the theorists of Socialist Realism. Anyone who thinks that art has some moral effect is likely to think that representational art, because of its moral content, has a particularly important moral effect. Although Plato does discuss the effects of music, his main concern is the moral impact of literature. Similarly, Socialist Realism in Soviet Russia has paid some attention to music but the main stress has been on literature and films.

Before we discuss in more detail some views of the relationship between art and morality, one other general question must be raised: what counts as morality? When morality is mentioned people often think first of a moral code, of rules about not murdering and not stealing, or about keeping promises and giving money to charity. They think of a code which governs our relationships with others. It is also possible to think of morality not in terms of rules but in terms of virtues. Morality, we might say, is about kindness, or generosity, or honesty. To conform with morality is to be a certain sort of person, not just to perform certain types of action. Morality is relevant to art in both these senses. The people in a film, a play, or a novel may be depicted as breaking moral rules or as conforming to them. They will also be depicted as people of a certain sort. As we have already seen, the representation of character plays an important part in both literature and films and morality as a matter of virtues may well be more relevant to the moral content of such works than morality as a matter of rules. Sometimes 'morality' is used more widely to refer to a general outlook on life and an overall scheme of values rather than specifically to moral rules or moral virtues. So we might speak of someone's moral outlook when concerned with his or her attitude to friends and family, to a career, to serious illness, or to death. Often discussions of the relationship between art and morality are concerned not with moral rules but with virtues and moral character or even with a general moral outlook. These different uses of the term 'morality' must be kept in mind as we examine some of the views that have been held.

In the modern world it is common to assume that art has at least some degree of autonomy, that it exists in a sphere of its own and is to be judged in the first instance by values and standards peculiar to it. We already imply this by making a distinction between the aesthetic and the moral, even if we go on to trace connections between art and morality. In the ancient world no such assumption was made. On the contrary, it was taken for granted that poets were teachers and that art had moral effects on its audience. We also distinguish between the moral and the political, between our dealings with one another as individuals and our role as citizens of a state. The ancients did not make such a sharp distinction. They therefore assumed that the effects of art were important politically as well as morally.[3] These assumptions are most clearly developed in the work of Plato. In *Republic* II and III Plato expounds his view of the role of art, and in particular the role of literature, in educating the future rulers of his ideal state. He sees a simple and direct connection between the moral content of a work and its moral effect. Passages in Homer which represent the heroes as fearful or self-indulgent, for example, are to be banned because their readers will enter into the emotions of the fictional characters and thus will themselves become fearful and self-indulgent. Conversely, Plato approves of passages which show the heroes displaying courage and self-control because they encourage the development of these qualities.[4] Elsewhere Plato stresses the power of art to arouse the emotions.[5] This explains the importance he attaches to art's moral impact. In his view we have no control over our reactions to art. The effect is immediate and powerful, incapable of direction by reason and the intellect. This is why Plato sees art as positively dangerous and proposes that in his ideal state it should be subject to severe censorship.

Plato's view of the effects of art is in some ways quite close to the view of a much more recent writer discussed earlier in this book, Tolstoy. For Tolstoy, as for Plato, art has an immediate effect on the emotions of its audience and this emotional effect is of moral significance. Only art which communicates brotherly love and the simple feelings of common life is really good. Art which communicates morally reprehensible feelings such as pride, sexual desire, and discontent with life is condemned. Like Plato, Tolstoy regards most of the art which was highly prized in his own time as pernicious. He even condemns most of his own previous work, including his two greatest novels, *War and Peace* and *Anna Karenina*. He argues that both art and artists must change if the moral potential of art is to be realized. However, Tolstoy differs from Plato in setting his view in a less clearly political context. Although he is concerned with what a human community should be like, *What is Art?* does not describe an ideal state as Plato's *Republic* does. More importantly, Tolstoy differs from Plato in his account of the moral content of art. Plato, who holds that art is imitation,[6] sees the moral content in what is represented and particularly in the types of character portrayed. Tolstoy, who holds a simple expression theory, constantly describes the moral content of art in terms of feeling. Whereas Plato would say that reading about a self-indulgent character, or seeing a self-indulgent character portrayed on stage, will make me into a self-indulgent person, Tolstoy would say that the writer who depicts a self-indulgent character is given to self-indulgence and through his work infects the reader with his own feelings.

Both Plato and Tolstoy think that the kind of art we are exposed to can affect the kind of people we become. They are concerned with moral character rather than with moral rules. They do not suppose that reading one violent book or watching one violent play will make me go out and perform a violent act. What they do think is that the continuous reading of violent books or prolonged exposure to violent plays will make me become the kind of person who is liable to commit violent acts. (I have referred to plays rather than films here to avoid anachronism but their views would of course apply to films in exactly the same way.)

Plato and Tolstoy both assume that it can be firmly established that certain works have certain effects. Plato is sure that the representation of cowardly people makes us cowardly; the only way to prevent this effect is to suppress such representations. Tolstoy is confident that the artist who sincerely expresses feelings of pride will pass those feelings on to us; we can no more escape than we could escape an infectious disease and the infection can only be prevented by taking care that we are not exposed to the disease in the first place. In fact, however, the effects of art are neither so certain nor so direct. People vary a great deal both in the intensity of their response to art and in the form which that response takes. It may well be true that some people become more liable to violent acts if they watch violent films but other reactions are also possible. Some people may indulge fantasies of violence by watching a film instead of working out those fantasies in real life. Others may be simply repelled by even glamorous representations of violence. Still others may be left unmoved, neither attracted nor repelled.

Although Plato and Tolstoy speak in terms which suggest that the moral effects of art are automatic and inevitable, their views would still be persuasive if it could be shown that certain works had morally corrupting or improving effects not on everybody but on most people. If it could be shown that few people are impervious to the corrupting effects of violence in films, there would be a good case for banning such films. But it is difficult to show even this. The only satisfactory way to do it would be a prolonged sociological and psychological experiment, involving the study of large numbers of people, over a long period of time. Such a study would have to take account of all the other factors of inherited temperament, social background, and education which contribute to the formation of character, endeavouring to weigh these against the effects of violent films. The same problem arises in debates over obscenity in art. In English law 'obscene' is defined as 'tending to deprave and corrupt'. 'Tending' means that only a likely effect on most people needs to be proved, not an inevitable effect on everybody. Even so, it is notoriously hard to prove that particular works of art do tend to deprave and corrupt. The Williams Report on Obscenity and Film Censorship pointed out that the considerable amount of psychological research which has been done on the effects of obscene or violent visual material has produced only inconclusive results.

Faced with the difficulty of assessing the effects of obscenity or violence on people's characters, we might be tempted to fall back after all on counting depraved actions. We might suppose, for example, that counting crimes of violence to see if they increased after A Clockwork Orange was released would give us some information about the effects of that film. In fact, as the Williams Report shows, such statistical evidence is subject to many problems. We have to decide what counts as a crime of violence, we have to bear in mind that an increase in the number of crimes reported does not necessarily reflect an increase in the number of crimes committed, and we must realize that even if crimes of violence did increase after the release of a particular film, it does not follow that that film was the cause. In any case, the statistical evidence available is no more conclusive than the evidence from psychological research. Because it is so hard to assess whether works of art, or even items of crude pornography, are corrupting, the Williams Committee proposed that the notion of 'tending to deprave and corrupt' be excluded from English law and be replaced by a test of what is 'offensive to reasonable people', although this recommendation has not so far been put into effect.[7]

It is just as difficult to assess whether good art has a morally improving effect. On the one hand aesthetic excellence is no guarantee of good moral effects: it is often pointed out that some Nazis were highly cultivated people and that the excellence of German art, music, and literature did nothing to save German society from moral corruption in the 1930s and 1940s.[8] On the other hand, it may be doubted whether art with good moral content really improves its audience either. We cannot make simple generalizations about the moral effects of art.

Discussions of censorship often focus on the question whether any art should be banned. Plato, however, advocates not only the banning of art which would be morally corrupting but the encouragement of art which would be morally improving. Tolstoy looks towards an art of the future which will transmit worthwhile feelings to all. Both Plato and Tolstoy approve of art which promotes the right moral values. But it is not as easy as Plato and Tolstoy imply to produce such art. For one thing, as we have just seen, we cannot be certain of the improving effects of art, any more than of its corrupting effects. In addition, there is much more to a work of art than its moral content or an attempt to produce moral effects. The common distinction between art and propaganda is made because successful art has a richness and complexity which often belies any simple moral or political message. Thus Virgil's *Aeneid* is to some degree propaganda for the regime of the Emperor Augustus. It exalts the values of duty and patriotism that the regime sought to promote and presents the Augustan settlement after the Civil Wars as the culmination of

Roman history, foreshadowed in the legendary founding of
Rome by Aeneas. Yet at the same time the poem shows us the
obverse of the Augustan values, for Aeneas founds Rome only at
considerable cost: he has to abandon Dido and when he arrives in
Italy he is forced to fight a damaging war against the native
inhabitants whose champion, Turnus, is presented as a heroic
figure. The poem ends with the death of Turnus not with the
foundation of Aeneas' city. I mentioned earlier that Tolstoy in
What is Art? condemns most of his own previous work, including
War and Peace and *Anna Karenina*. The only works of his own
which he is there prepared to regard as acceptable are two slight
and simple short stories, *God Sees the Truth but Waits* and *The
Prisoner of the Caucasus*. These stories may promote the right
moral values but most of us would prize *War and Peace* and
Anna Karenina far more highly because of their superior
aesthetic value.

The simple accounts of the relationship between art and morals
offered by Plato and Tolstoy can accommodate neither the difficulty of proving that a given work of art has good or bad moral
effects nor the fact that art is not simple propaganda. This need
not mean that we rush to the other extreme and deny that art can
have any moral effects whatever. I propose now to examine two
more sophisticated positions which grant art a considerable
degree of autonomy without denying a relationship between art
and morals. The first of these is the Marxist position, the second
the position adumbrated by Matthew Arnold and more fully
expressed in the literary criticism of F. R. Leavis. As we shall see
these two positions differ greatly, not only in the account they
offer of the relationship between art and morals but in what they
include under the term 'morality'. I shall begin by considering the
Marxist position.

It is in some ways misleading to speak of 'the' Marxist position
on this topic, for there are many different Marxist views of art. I
have space to discuss only a few of these.[9] It is also a little misleading to refer to the Marxist position on the relationship
between art and morals because for a Marxist morals cannot
properly be considered apart from the social, political, and economic structures in which people live. Marxism has revived the
ancient Greek view that morals and politics are indissolubly connected so that for a Marxist morality is not a code, nor a set of

virtues, nor a general outlook on life, but only one aspect of the life of human beings in society. Marxist theories of art therefore offer not so much a view of the relationship between art and morals as a view of the relationship between art and the social and political structure which includes morals.

Fundamental to all Marxist views of art is a distinction between the economic base of society and the superstructure. To the base belong the production of goods and the relationships between people which are required by the mode of production at a particular time, such as the relationship between capitalist and proletarian; to the superstructure belong not only the legal and political institutions which keep the mode of production in being but also a society's beliefs about itself, its ideology. For a Marxist art is part of ideology.[10] Marxists recognize that ideology takes many forms and that its relationship to the economic base of society may be quite complex. As part of ideology and part of the superstructure, art has 'relative autonomy'. Thus a Marxist can acknowledge the importance of artistic forms and conventions but believes that ultimately there is a relationship between those forms and conventions and the economic base. Different Marxist views of the relationship between superstructure and base produce different accounts of the relationship between art and social and economic reality. At its simplest Marxism sees the superstructure as reflecting the base and art as reflecting social and economic reality. On such a view the moral and political content of art reflects the society in which the art has been produced. This view may be combined with a view of the effects of art not unlike Plato's and Tolstoy's, that art with the right kind of moral and political content will help encourage the building of the right kind of society. It is this straightforward Marxist view which has been put into political practice as Socialist Realism in both Russia and China.

It is no easier for artists to produce work of aesthetic value according to the canons of Socialist Realism than it was for Roman poets to conform with the moral and political ideals of the Emperor Augustus. Moreover, the simple view that art reflects social and economic reality, although it can offer reasonably satisfying accounts of realistic art forms such as the nineteenth-century novel, cannot cope satisfactorily with modernist art. This weakness is evident in the work of George Lukács.

Lukács did not go all the way with Socialist Realism but he did regard art as reflecting the society in which it was created and tended to treat the realistic novel of the first half of the nineteenth century as a literary ideal. He criticized innovative twentieth-century writers such as James Joyce, Franz Kafka, and Samuel Beckett for their experimental methods and for the despairing, nihilist outlook which he believed those methods expressed.[11]

The limitations of Lukács's approach were keenly felt by Brecht as an artist committed to Marxism who sought to put that commitment into practice in his art. As a dramatist Brecht was concerned with the effect of his plays on the audience and he developed his own theory of 'epic theatre'. In Brecht's view, in traditional 'dramatic theatre' the audience are encouraged to enter into the emotions expressed by the actors. Temporarily taken in by the dramatic illusion they are lulled into acceptance of what they see presented on the stage. By contrast, the epic theatre encourages the audience to be conscious observers, always aware that they are watching a play. They are thus forced to think about what they see so that they leave the theatre roused to take action and change the world.[12]

Brecht considers art from the point of view of a dramatist active in writing and putting on plays. The view that art simply reflects social and economic reality has also been rejected by a number of Marxist critics whose appreciation of art has led them to stress its relative autonomy. Pierre Macherey, for example, has developed the idea that the artist is not so much a creator as a producer. Rather than creating a unified and coherent whole he or she produces something which is necessarily incomplete, which suffers from the same contradictions as the prevailing ideology. We discover the social reality by investigating what the author does *not* say, by seeing which aspects of reality are left out of the text.[13] Macherey's ideas have been taken further by Terry Eagleton.[14] Such an approach makes it possible for a Marxist to interpret a much wider range of literary texts but the reader is still constrained to see in every text some relationship to reality as Marxists understand it.

Macherey is primarily concerned with the ideological content of a text rather than its effects on its readers. Eagleton, however, also believes that literary works can have the effect of promoting ideology. In a book on Richardson's *Clarissa* he analyses that novel as exemplifying bourgeois ideology and at the same time unwittingly exposing its contradictions. In the introduction he draws attention to the way in which Richardson's novels succeeded in promoting bourgeois ideology by their popularity. He sees a parallel between Richardson's work and Brecht's epic theatre and comments ironically:

The delight Richardson took in hearing that one of his works had persuaded a reader to mend his dissolute ways can now only be thought naïve: 'art' is supposed to affect 'life' of course, but not in such embarrassingly direct ways. . . . One can be sure that most of those who find Richardson's delight naïve would also find a drama which incited its audience of sweated labourers to strike incorrigibly vulgar.[15]

Yet Eagleton does not clearly relate this to his analysis of *Clarissa* as exposing the contradictions of bourgeois ideology and his mention of 'vulgarity' is beside the point. One might or might not consider a drama which incited its audience to strike to be a good play. That would depend on such matters as the play's construction, the depiction of the characters, and the use of language. The dramatic power of the play might indeed help it to bring about a strike but given the right political and social conditions a play could have this effect without being good as a play.

In any case, if I wanted to incite sweated labourers to strike, I am not sure that putting on a Brechtian play would be the most effective method. I could distribute a pamphlet, or make a speech, to the labourers pointing out their oppression and urging them to throw it off. I could seek out possible leaders of a strike and encourage them to approach their fellows individually and so spread the word without publicity. These are the methods employed by political activists and beside them the arts can play at most an ancillary and subordinate role. It is an illusion to suppose otherwise.

Marxists have developed sophisticated theories of the relationship between the content of literature and social reality but they have not yet developed an equally sophisticated account of the social and political effects of literature. Marxist analyses of content can help us to appreciate some works: whatever Lukács's weaknesses as a theorist his interpretations of Balzac's novels reveal aspects of those novels which might not be perceived by a casual reader. His interpretations are supported by the text of the novels and do not conflict with the criteria of author's intentions and audience's expectations when these are understood in the terms I argued for in Chapter 7. Yet other works are forced by a Marxist analysis into a mould which they do not fit. In *Criticism and Ideology* Terry Eagleton offers a brief account of *Middlemarch* which sees all the characters as types and dissolves George Eliot's concern with the moral dilemmas confronting individual people into theoretical problems about the expression of ideology. Rather than revealing aspects of *Middlemarch* which the reader might otherwise have missed, this account simply obscures our understanding of the novel.[16] If one is not a committed Marxist there is no reason to interpret every work of literature as related to a Marxist understanding of reality. Attempts to do so risk forcing the text and ignoring both the author's intentions and the original audience's expectations.

Quite a different approach to the relationship between art and morals has been taken by English literary critics writing in the tradition of Matthew Arnold. Arnold in his essay on 'The Study of Poetry' claimed that poetry would come to replace religion and philosophy: 'More and more mankind will discover that we have to turn to poetry to interpret life for us, to console us, to sustain us.'[17] The poetry which is best from an aesthetic point of view is also the poetry that can best perform this function. It becomes clear later in the essay that for Arnold aesthetic and moral value go together:

the substance and character of the best poetry acquire their special character from possessing, in an eminent degree, truth and seriousness . . . The superior character of truth and seriousness, in the matter and substance of the best poetry, is inseparable from the superiority of diction and movement marking its style and manner.[18]

Arnold proceeds to a brief survey of English poetry from Chaucer to the eighteenth century. It is evident from that survey that the marks of the best poetry are 'high seriousness' and 'absolute sincerity'. The poetry of Chaucer and the best of Robert Burns are admitted only to the second rank because they lack high seriousness although the view of life expressed is 'large, free . . . kindly'. Since Arnold's concern is mainly with lyric poetry he sees the moral content of poetry not in the characters or actions represented but in the view of life expressed. The moral effect of poetry and its religious effect go closely together. Poetry offers not so much moral improvement as the kind of consolation and understanding of life formerly afforded by religion.

Arnold's desire to assign to poetry the function of religion looks dated to us now and the weaknesses of his view of religion stand out clearly. He envisages religion as simply a means of finding consolation for the stresses and difficulties of life, ignoring questions about the existence of God or his relationship with man. More relevant to the present discussion is Arnold's view of morality. He is not concerned with a moral code, nor with moral virtues in the usual sense. His concern is with a poet's general outlook on life. A person's general outlook on life reflects his or her character. The qualities Arnold praises in the poets he values most highly are the qualities of character he finds expressed in their work. These qualities of high seriousness, sincerity, largeness of view, and kindliness form, by implication, a list of virtues. It is an odd list of virtues, however, in that, with the exception of kindliness, these qualities involve relatively little in the way of action affecting other people. One can sit at home in an armchair and be full of high seriousness and sincerity, taking a large view of life, while outside people go without food or shelter. If we considered only Arnold's activity as a poet and critic we might suppose that he sat at home reading and writing and ignored the social problems of Victorian England. This is far from the truth. As a hard-working Inspector of Schools Arnold helped to improve education for working-class children. It would be quite wrong to assume that high seriousness, sincerity, and the rest were the only qualities he prized. What he did think was that these were the qualities which mattered in poetry. Poetry cannot feed the hungry, find people homes, or provide them with schools. What it can do, in Arnold's view, is express certain noble states of mind.

Arnold very properly insists that the force of his generalities lies in their application to specific examples. Nevertheless, he offers little detailed analysis of the lines of poetry he cites as examples of the best in both substance and manner. As a result his critical judgements appear subjective and his virtues of high seriousness and sincerity, largeness of view and kindliness, remain vague and undefined. A not dissimilar moral and aesthetic outlook was combined with a much more penetrating criticism of individual works of literature by F. R. Leavis. Leavis couples together aesthetic and moral considerations in a way very reminiscent of Arnold in the introduction to his study of the novels of George Eliot, Henry James, and Joseph Conrad, *The Great Tradition*. In that introduction he presents Jane Austen as the important precursor for these three novelists and insists that in Jane Austen's work aesthetic value and moral significance cannot be separated:

when we examine the formal perfection of *Emma*, we find that it can be appreciated only in terms of the moral preoccupations that characterize the novelist's peculiar interest in life. Those who suppose it to be an 'aesthetic matter', a beauty of 'composition' that is combined, miraculously, with 'truth to life', can give no adequate reason for the view that *Emma* is a great novel and no intelligent account of its perfection of form.[19]

It is not surprising that Leavis's moral criteria emerge clearly in a book on the novel, a literary form which is high in moral content. Moral criteria are most evident in his chapter on George Eliot, a novelist whose own moral interests are made quite plain in her novels. Nevertheless, a similar coupling of aesthetic and moral values appears in Leavis's criticism of poetry too. The works that Leavis values highly are regularly described as 'mature', they possess 'intense moral seriousness' and exhibit self-knowledge. The works he regards as lacking in value are described as sentimental; they display not self-knowledge but self-pity. In *Revaluation*, for example, he uses these terms to praise Wordsworth and Keats while condemning Shelley.[20] Besides maturity and self-knowledge Leavis values what he calls 'life'. Thus in *The Great Tradition* Henry James's later work is criticized for being deficient in 'full-bodied life'. Leavis explicitly connects this with the 'moral unsatisfactoriness' he finds in *The Golden Bowl*, in which, in his view, Maggie and Adam Verver with their collector's attitude to other people are too sympathetically presented.[21] So, too, in *Revaluation* Leavis distinguishes between the aestheticism of Keats and the aestheticism of Dante Gabriel Rossetti and Lionel Johnson: 'Keats's aestheticism . . . does not mean any such cutting off of the special valued order of experience from direct, vulgar living ("Live!—our servants will do that for us") as is implied in the aesthetic antithesis of

Art and Life.'[22] It was this quality of 'life' which Leavis particularly valued in D. H. Lawrence.

The virtues of maturity, self-knowledge, and moral seriousness are all 'armchair' virtues, even more so than the virtues Arnold finds in the best poetry. Leavis's valuing of 'full-bodied life' stresses the importance of going out and doing things but gives little guide as to what one is to do. Value is placed on deep experience by the individual rather than on any actions involving others. The self-centredness of Leavis's approach comes out in his talk of spiritual health and sickness. To promote our spiritual health we must seek to become more mature and self-aware, less prone to self-pity and sentimentality. Leavis sometimes implies that if we understand ourselves better, we shall understand all humanity better and his criticism of *The Golden Bowl* does suggest a connection between the absence of 'full-bodied life' and a tendency to treat other people as objects. However, he never spells out just how spiritual health affects our relations with others. He takes it for granted that if we are mature, self-aware, unsentimental, and avoid excessive aestheticism, then we shall be better people. In his defence, as in Arnold's, it might perhaps be said that there is a greater likelihood of literature making us more mature and self-aware than of literature making us more honest or more charitable or more active in changing the world. Two serious difficulties remain. First, Leavis simply assumes that literature with mature and self-aware content will have the effect of making us mature and self-aware. His occasional comments about the effects of literature, such as the remark in *The Great Tradition* that George Eliot is 'a peculiarly fortifying and wholesome author',[23] do not suggest any profound reflection on the problems of assessing the moral effect of literature. Secondly, even if good literature does make us mature, self-aware, and spiritually healthy, if it cannot be shown to make us better people in any other sense, its effects are not after all of much moral importance. If maturity and self-awareness do not make us more honest or more charitable, more inclined to feed the starving or shelter the homeless, then why not just acknowledge that the value we find in literature and the other arts is remote from moral value in any significant sense of 'moral'? It is true that if one takes the ultimate aim of morality to be the spiritual purity and wholeness of the individual, then literature which makes us more mature and self-aware will be contributing to our moral improvement. In my view, however, relationships with others are central to morality and we cannot save our own souls unless we improve the world around us.[24]

None of the views discussed so far examines the moral effect of literature in any great detail. On the one hand, we have Arnold's claim that the poetry of high seriousness will console and sustain us. In Leavis's hands this becomes an assumption that mature, self-aware literature will make us mature, self-aware people. On the other hand, both Marxists, who grant literature relative autonomy, and Plato and Tolstoy, who make no distinction between the aesthetic and the moral, give literature a powerful role in inculcating values and attitudes, whether to promote an ideology or to change our moral character. Both groups of views make high claims for the power of art, claims which are probably too high. Yet there is some truth in a more modest and modified version of each.

In the last chapter I argued that literature shows us how things might be. This account indicates the way in which the view of Arnold and Leavis should be modified. Literature presents us with a view of the world and good literature presents its view successfully or effectively. Purely literary standards will not tell us that the world of *The Golden Bowl* is less true than the world of *Middlemarch*, will not tell us to see the world as George Eliot saw it rather than as the ageing Henry James saw it. A successful literary presentation enables us to see the world from the point of view of that presentation. In novels and drama we are shown the world from the different points of view of the various characters and this helps us to understand what these different kinds of people are like. Reading *Middlemarch* helps us to understand people like Dorothea and Lydgate. It may also help us to understand ourselves since Dorothea and Lydgate, like us, are human beings, but we come to such understanding of ourselves through understanding the fictional others. In the same way reading *The Golden Bowl* helps us to understand people like the Ververs. James is not necessarily asking us to approve of them. He is asking us to see things from their point of view for a while. In lyric poetry there is only one point of view, that expressed by the poet as speaker of the poem. As a result we are likely to feel that in appreciating Keats's 'Ode to Autumn' we are coming to understand Keats. Care is needed here. All we are coming to understand is the point of view expressed in the poem. It may or may not be a point of view constantly maintained by the real person, John Keats. In any case, the point of view need not be one we believe to be correct and coming to understand the view of how things might be presented in the poem is more like coming to understand somebody else than like coming to understand ourselves.

The claim is often made that the moral value of art lies in its ability to give us imaginative insight into other people. My account of literature as showing how things might be supports this claim.[25] What, it might be asked, has imaginative insight to do with morality? The answer is that a better understanding of other people contributes to the development of moral virtues. We shall be both kinder and fairer in our treatment of others if we understand them better. Understanding ourselves and understanding others are connected since as human beings we all have things in common. Moreover, if we understand ourselves we may be more capable of effective moral action. Nevertheless, in morality understanding ourselves is less important than understanding others. Arnold's view that poetry can console and sustain us and Leavis's stress on maturity and self-awareness suggest a misleading account of what literature can do and a skewed picture of morality. If we amend their account to say that literature can give us insight into others as well as ourselves, then we can see one way in which aesthetically good literature is also of moral value.

If we regard literature as giving us insight into others, we must recognize that it might enable us to see the world from the point of view of those who are evil and corrupt and so might lead us to sympathize with them. 'Tout comprendre c'est tout pardonner', as the saying goes. What worried Plato about the power of literature was precisely that it might bring us to sympathize too much with the wicked and that such sympathy would in the end make us become like them. Earlier in this chapter I stressed the difficulty of assessing whether art really can change our characters. Although Plato and Tolstoy exaggerate the extent to which this is possible, I would not deny that art has some part to play in inculcating values and attitudes, for it can influence the terms in which we see life. Violent films, for example, can inculcate an attitude which regards violence as an appropriate response to threat or injury and a value system in which people who commit acts of violence are seen as glamorous and courageous. Such effects are not inevitable since we bring previously formed attitudes into the cinema with us and an initial aversion to violence may well persist and modify or overcome the influence of a violent film.

The effect of works of art on values and attitudes is often subtle, indirect, and only appreciated with hindsight. Admittedly there are some celebrated instances of highly successful works having an immediate effect. Goethe's novel, *The Sorrows of Young Werther*, whose sensitive hero ends by committing suicide, made many young men fancy themselves Werthers in real life, sometimes with disastrous consequences. However, the relationship between art and the values and attitudes of real life is not usually so direct. A more typical example is provided by the English poetry of the First World War. The patriotic poetry written at the beginning of the war by Rupert Brooke and others gave way to the very different poetry of Wilfred Owen and Siegfried Sassoon. The change reflected a change in the attitudes of the fighting men from jingoistic patriotism to an awareness of the futility of war. In turn the poetry of Owen and Sassoon impressed that futility upon its readers and contributed to a fundamental change in the attitudes to war of combatant and non-combatant alike. C. Day Lewis, who was born in 1904 and so was too young to take part in the war, valued Owen in particular for just this reason. In his introduction to Owen's *Collected Poems* he wrote: 'it is Owen . . . whose poetry came home deepest to my own generation, so that we could never again think of war as anything but a vile, if necessary, evil.'[26]

If we recognize that art can influence our values and attitudes, should we then advocate censorship? The effect of art on mature adults is reduced by the fact that their characters are already largely formed. It has a far more powerful influence on children and adolescents whose moral characters are still developing. Most parents and teachers wish to control to some extent the influences to which young people in their charge are exposed. It may be more appropriate for parents and teachers to advise children and adolescents on what they should see, hear, and read than for the state or other authority to do so. Nevertheless, a limited amount of censorship, such as the present practice in Britain of restricting the age-group to which a film may be shown, does seem to me justified.

Where adults are concerned the issue is more difficult. A work's aesthetic value may be held to outweigh a possible corrupting moral influence, particularly when we bear in mind the difficulties of assessing such an influence. In addition, other values come into play. Censorship restricts freedom of expression and we may well feel that a society in which artists are free to create what they please is a better society than one in which the citizens are protected from what might be evil influences. Mature adults do have some control over their reactions to art. I can choose not to go to *A Clockwork Orange*. If I do go, I can consciously try to detach myself from becoming involved with the film, or I can subsequently counteract its impact by reminding myself of my previous disapproval of violence. The case for censorship is much weaker than Plato thought, not only because freedom of expression is valuable but also because the effects of art are neither so sure nor so direct nor so irresistible as he believed.

Works of art are not isolated from the artists who produce them, from the world which provides their material, or from the audience to whom they are presented. At the same time they do not stand in any simple and direct relationship to artist, world, or audience, since the artist's experiences and the material offered by the world are reshaped into an artistic form and the audience responds to the form as well as the content of a work. If we return to the question with which this book began, 'Why bother about art?', we are now in a position to offer some answer.

First of all, both art and natural beauty have value in themselves. However good our standard of living, however perfect our social arrangements, however upright our way of life, our lives will be poorer and more limited if we lack opportunities for aesthetic appreciation. In addition, art does have a certain moral value. It is no use pretending that art can change the world directly or can automatically transform our characters. Art can have a moral influence by giving us imaginative insight into other people and by inculcating values and attitudes, often in subtle and indirect ways. Just because the effect of art on our values and attitudes is subtle and indirect it is easy not to be aware of it. We can become more aware of it if we study works of art with some care and if we reflect on our aesthetic experience. The formal study of literature, art, and music is worthwhile not only because it enriches our aesthetic experience but because like any other formal study it provides training in intellectual discipline and rational reflection. Enriching our aesthetic experience goes together with developing our powers of imagination and understanding. Art engages both the emotions and the intellect and the study of art requires a combination of imaginative flexibility and intellectual discipline. If we develop our ability to respond to art we shall develop our potential as human beings.

Notes

The following frequently cited works are referred to in the notes in abbreviated form:

Kant   I. Kant, *Critique of Aesthetic Judgement* (trans. J. C. Meredith, Oxford, 1952).

Margolis   J. Margolis (ed.), *Philosophy Looks at the Arts* (revised edn., Temple University, Pa., 1978).

Osborne   H. Osborne (ed.), *Aesthetics* (Oxford Readings in Philosophy, Oxford, 1972).

Savile   A. Savile, *The Test of Time* (Oxford, 1982).

Chapter 2: Imitation

1. Plato, *Republic* X, 596e, trans. G. M A. Grube.
2. Plato, *Symposium*, 201-12 presents the view that physical beauty can spur its lover on to the Form of Beauty. This contributed to Platonist modifications of Plato's own theory regarding art. See, for example, Cicero, *Orator*, 2. 8-3. 10 (the artist imitates a Form in his own mind); Plotinus, *Ennead*, v. 8. 1 (the artist imitates an ideal, transcendent Form). For the weaker version, that the artist imitates a general idea, see, for example, Sir Joshua Reynolds, *Ninth Discourse on Art*. For further references and discussion of this whole subject, see E. Panofsky, *Idea: A Concept in Art Theory*, trans. J. J. S. Peake (New York, 1968) and M. H. Abrams, *The Mirror and the Lamp* (Oxford, 1953), ch. 2.
3. For Raphael, see Panofsky, op. cit., pp. 59-60. On the Michelangelo poem (XCIV), see R. J. Clements, *Michelangelo's Theory of Art* (New York, 1961), pp. 14 ff.
4. *Don Juan*, Canto II, Stanza 118.
5. 2nd edn., Indianapolis, 1976.
6. Esp. in Chapter 7.
7. *Philosophical Investigations*, II, xi.
8. This is denied by E. H. Gombrich, in *Art and Illusion* (London, 1960), but maintained by R. Wollheim, against Gombrich, in 'On Drawing an Object' pp. 22 ff. (Inaugural lecture, London, 1964; reprinted in Osborne, pp. 121-44 and in Margolis, pp. 249-72.) Both views are persuasively argued, but in the end it is Wollheim who seems to me to be correct.
9. See R. Wollheim, *Art and its Objects* (2nd edn., Cambridge, 1980),

supplementary essay 5, 'Seeing-as, seeing-in and pictorial representation'. Cf. also R. Scruton, *Art and Imagination* (London, 1974), ch. 13.

Chapter 3: Expression

1. On this great shift in outlook in the Romantic period, see M. H. Abrams, *The Mirror and the Lamp* (Oxford, 1953). For the ancient roots cf expression theory, see esp. 'Longinus', *On the Sublime*.
2. Wordsworth's Preface was first published with the second edition of *Lyrical Ballads* (1800). Eliot defines the objective correlative in this way in his essay, 'Hamlet and his Problems', in *The Sacred Wood* (London, 1920).
3. *Essay on the True Art of Playing Keyboard Instruments*, trans. W. J. Mitchell (London, 1949), p. 152.
4. For further discussion of Tolstoy's view of the moral effects of art, see Chapter 9.
5. See esp. Kant, §. 2, and the other writers discussed in Chapter 5.
6. See R. G. Collingwood, *The Principles of Art* (Oxford, 1938), pp. 130–5.
7. For further discussion of the relationship between the artist's intentions and the diverse interpretations of the audience, see Chapter 7.
8. For a sensitive treatment of this point, see R. K. Elliott, 'Aesthetic Theory and the Experience of Art', *Proceedings of the Aristotelian Society*, 67 (1966–7), 111–26, reprinted in Osborne, pp. 145–57 and in Margolis, pp. 45–57.
9. Aristotle, *Poetics*, ch. 4, 1448b 15–17.
10. For a lively discussion of this and other points about 'sad music', see O. K. Bouwsma, 'The Expression Theory of Art' in M. Black (ed.), *Philosophical Analysis* (Ithaca, 1950), pp. 75–101, reprinted in W. Elton (ed.), *Aesthetics and Language* (Oxford, 1954), pp. 73–99.
11. e.g. Bouwsma, art. cit.; R. Wollheim, *Art and its Objects* (2nd edn., Cambridge, 1980), §§. 14–19.
12. Cf. the views of Eduard Hanslick and Susanne Langer discussed in Chapter 4.
13. The idea that our emotional response to works of art is an imagined one is developed in a different way by K. Walton, 'Fearing Fictions', *Journal of Philosophy*, 75 (1978), 5–27.

Chapter 4: Form

1. See Pliny the Elder, *Natural History*, 34. 55 and G. Richter, *A Handbook of Greek Art* (7th edn., London and New York, 1974), p. 120.

2. See R. Wittkower, *Architectural Principles in the Age of Humanism* (3rd edn., London, 1962), esp. Parts III and IV.
3. See, e.g., T. Todorov, *The Poetics of Prose* (Oxford, 1977), a translation of *Poétique de la prose* (Paris, 1971), esp. pp. 247 ff. Cf. D. Lodge, *The Modes of Modern Writing* (London, 1977), pp. 57 ff., and on Russian formalism A. Jefferson and D. Robey (eds.), *Modern Literary Theory* (2nd edn., London, 1986), ch. 1 and F. Jameson, *The Prison-House of Language* (Princeton, 1972), pp. 43 ff.
4. See Todorov, op. cit., ch. 10. Todorov's approach also produces a thought-provoking discussion of Benjamin Constant's *Adolphe* in ch. 7 but is much less convincing when applied to Homer's *Odyssey* in ch. 4.
5. For a clear short account of Derrida, see the essay by Jonathan Culler in J. Sturrock (ed.), *Structuralism and Since from Lévi-Strauss to Derrida* (Oxford, 1979) and for a more extended discussion, J. Culler, *On Deconstruction* (London, 1983), ch. 2.
6. See Kant, §§. 14 and 16; also §§. 4 and 23; for further discussion of Kant's views, see Chapter 5.
7. E. Hanslick, *The Beautiful in Music* (trans. G. Cohen; New York, 1957), pp. 21 and 23.
8. Ibid., pp. 29–30. Cf. Kant's inclusion of 'all music that is not set to words' among his examples of free beauty (Kant, §. 16).
9. Op. cit., pp. 40–1.
10. See 'An Essay in Aesthetics' and 'Retrospect' in *Vision and Design* (London, 1920), pp. 11–25 and 188–99 respectively, and *Transformations* (London, 1926), ch. 1, 'Some Questions in Esthetics'; for Fry's criticism of Bell, see *Vision and Design*, p. 195.
11. See Fry's recognition of this point in *Vision and Design*, p. 195.
12. For a discussion of this point by a psychologist, see R. Arnheim, *Art and Visual Perception* (London, 1956), ch. 1, esp. pp. 22 ff. on Cézanne's painting, *Madame Cézanne in a Yellow Chair*.
13. *Art* (London, 1914), p. 49.
14. *Vision and Design*, p. 199.
15. Cambridge, Mass., 1942. See ch. 8. Langer's view of music there is clearly related to Hanslick's view, although her emphasis is different; cf. her remarks on Hanslick scattered through the chapter.
16. London, 1953. See esp. ch. 3.
17. See *Transformations*, pp. 6–43 on the mixing of the different arts and esp. the remarks on pp. 27 ff. about song and opera.
18. Cf. Chapter 3; also S. Langer, *Feeling and Form*, p. 389.
19. Bell, *Art*, pp. 30 ff. (music); pp. 153, 156–8 (literature). Fry, *Transformations*, pp. 6 ff.
20. Op. cit., ch. 6, pp. 104 ff.

21. *Vision and Design*, pp. 196–7.
22. D. Lodge, *Working with Structuralism* (Boston, London, and Henley, 1981), pp. 108 ff. On the structuralist concern with relationships, cf. Sturrock, op. cit., p. 56, and the example from Roland Barthes cited there.
23. *Transformations*, pp. 7 and 10.
24. M. C. Beardsley, *Aesthetics: Problems in the Philosophy of Criticism* (2nd edn., Indianapolis, 1981), pp. 456–70; also pp. 190–209.
25. *Poetics*, chs. 7 and 8; cf. Plato, *Phaedrus*, 264b–c.
26. See, e.g., the theory put forward by H. Osborne in *Theory of Beauty* (London, 1952), esp. ch. 5.

Chapter 5: Art, beauty, and aesthetic appreciation

1. See the myth told in *Timaeus*, 27c ff., about the making of the world by a divine craftsman, and cf. *Republic* X, 596–8.
2. See Kant, §§. 23–9.
3. Such an answer would parallel G. E. Moore's account of goodness: see *Principia Ethica* (Cambridge, 1903), esp. ch. 1. Moore's own view of beauty relates it to goodness. He describes the beautiful as 'that of which the admiring contemplation is good in itself' (ibid., p. 201).
4. For an approach to aesthetics in terms of a wide range of 'aesthetic concepts' and an attempted account of their relationship to 'non-aesthetic concepts', see F. Sibley, 'Aesthetic Concepts', *Philosophical Review*, 68 (1959), 421–50, reprinted with revisions in Margolis, pp. 64–87, and 'Aesthetic and Non-aesthetic', *Philosophical Review*, 74 (1965), 135–59. Sibley's position is succinctly criticized by R. Scruton, *Art and Imagination* (London, 1974), ch. 3. H. Osborne, *British Journal of Aesthetics*, 23 (1983), 113–17, sorts out some of the different categories of aesthetic terms.
5. The definition is Stoic in origin: see Cicero, *Tusculan Disputations*, iv. 31. It is effectively criticized by Plotinus, *Ennead*, i. 6. 1, but repeated in Augustine, *De Civitate Dei*, xxii. 19. For its use in the Middle Ages, see E. de Bruyne, *Études d'esthétique médiévale* (Bruges, 1946), vol. iii, ch. 2, esp. pp. 126–35 (on Robert Grosseteste), also p. 47 (Gilbert Foliot) and p. 50 (Baldwin of Canterbury). For its use in the Renaissance by Alberti, see Savile, p. 153, and cf. also the passage of Hume cited by Savile, p. 157.
6. These are alternative standard English translations of the German 'Zweckmässigkeit ohne Zweck'.
7. For more detail on this, see D. W. Crawford, *Kant's Aesthetic Theory* (Madison, Wisconsin, 1974), ch. 4.
8. See J. Stolnitz, 'On the Origins of Aesthetic Disinterestedness', *Journal of Aesthetics and Art Criticism*, 20 (1961–2), 131–43.

9. See *The World as Will and Representation*, trans. E. J. F. Payne (Indian Hills, Colorado, 1958), vol. i, bk. iii, esp. §§. 30–41, and vol. ii, Supplements to the Third Book, esp. chs. 29–31, or the older translation by R. B. Haldane and J. Kemp under the title *The World as Will and Idea* (London, 1883), vol. i, bk. iii, esp. pp. 219–74, and vol. iii, Supplements to the Third Book, esp. chs. 29–31.

10. See E. Bullough, ' "Psychical Distance" as a Factor in Art and an Aesthetic Principle' in E. M. Wilkinson (ed.), *Aesthetics: Lectures and Essays* (London, 1957), pp. 91–130.

11. See R. Ingarden, 'Aesthetic Experience and Aesthetic Object', *Philosophy and Phenomenological Research*, 21 (1960–1), 289–313.

12. Cf. Scruton, op. cit., pp. 143–8.

13. Cf. Plotinus, *Ennead*, i. 6 *passim*; G. Sircello, *A New Theory of Beauty* (Princeton, 1975), pp. 19–20; R. Ingarden, art. cit., pp. 295–7; Savile, p. 154.

14. On Kant's view of aesthetic disputes, see S. Körner, *Kant* (Harmondsworth, 1955), pp. 187–8 and Crawford, op. cit., pp. 164–71.

15. For some suggestions on how a Kantian account of these might be given, see D. W. Crawford, 'Comparative Aesthetic Judgements and Kant's Aesthetic Theory', *Journal of Aesthetics and Art Criticism*, 38 (1979–80), 289–98.

Chapter 6: Criticism, interpretation, and evaluation

1. Kant, §. 33.

2. Cf. *Poetics*, 1450b 26–33.

3. J. C. Maxwell's discussion in his Arden Shakespeare edition of *Titus Andronicus* (revised edn., London, 1968), pp. xxxii–xxxviii, makes interesting reading in this context.

4. *Poetics*, 1449b 12–13. See further H. House, *Aristotle's Poetics* (London, 1956), pp. 64–7.

5. The distinction is taken for granted by R. A. Sharpe, 'Interpreting Art', *Proceedings of the Aristotelian Society*, supp. vol. 55 (1981), 19–32, and criticized by E. Schaper in her reply in the same volume, 33–46. For a fuller discussion see S. H. Olsen, *The Structure of Literary Understanding* (Cambridge, 1978), chs. 4 and 5, and cf. also his 'Criticism and Appreciation' in P. Lamarque (ed.), *Philosophy and Fiction* (Aberdeen, 1983), pp. 38–51.

6. *The Anatomy of Criticism* (Princeton, 1957), p. 20. See also Frye's later essay 'On Value-Judgements' in *The Stubborn Structure* (London, 1970), pp. 66–73. Frye's view has recently been attacked by Anthony Savile (Savile, pp. 191–4). For a discussion of the same issue from a different point of view, cf. W. K. Wimsatt, *The Verbal Icon* (Lexington, Ky., 1954), pp. 235–51.

7. *Shakespeare: The Last Phase* (London, 1954), p. 261.
8. *A History of Western Art* (London, 1968), p. 134.
9. An extreme view of this kind is espoused by Stanley Fish in 'Demonstration vs. Persuasion: Two Models of Criticism' in P. Hernadi (ed.), *What is Criticism?* (Bloomington, Ind., 1981), pp. 30–7, an essay extracted from chs. 15 and 16 of his book *Is There a Text in this Class?: The Authority of Interpretive Communities* (Cambridge, Mass., 1980).
10. See Kathleen Raine, 'Who Made the Tyger?', *Encounter*, 2, no. 6 (June 1954), 43–50 and E. D. Hirsch, *Innocence and Experience* (New Haven and London, 1964), pp. 244–52. These two conflicting interpretations are cited by Stanley Fish, in the essay referred to in n. 9, in support of his view that what a critic sees in a text depends on his point of view, and that in offering an interpretation he seeks to persuade others to share his perspective.
11. *The Poetics of Prose* (Oxford, 1977), ch. 10.
12. *The Triple Thinkers* (revised edn., London, 1952), pp. 89–96, with pp. 121–2, further discussed in Chapter 8 below.
13. *Studies in European Realism* (London, 1950), ch. 1. For some further discussion of Marxist views of art, see Chapter 9.
14. *Pagan Mysteries in the Renaissance* (2nd edn., London, 1968), p. 131.

Chapter 7: Intentions and expectations

1. *Milton's Minor Poems* (London, 1969), ch. 9.
2. *Shakespeare: The Last Phase* (London, 1954), pp. 1–2.
3. In 'Tradition and the Individual Talent', *The Sacred Wood* (London, 1920).
4. 'The Intentional Fallacy', *Sewanee Review*, 54 (1946), 468–88, frequently reprinted, e.g., in W. K. Wimsatt, *The Verbal Icon* (Lexington, Ky., 1954), pp. 3–18, in Margolis, pp. 293–306, and in D. Newton-de Molina (ed.), *On Literary Intention* (Edinburgh, 1976), pp. 1–13. My page references to this article are to *On Literary Intention* which also offers a useful collection of contributions to the ensuing debate.
5. *On Literary Intention*, p. 1.
6. Ibid.
7. For intention in relation to action, see J. A. Passmore, 'Intentions', *Proceedings of the Aristotelian Society*, supp. vol. 29 (1955), 131–46; A. C. MacIntyre, *The Unconscious* (London and New York, 1958), ch. 4; G. E. M. Anscombe, *Intention* (Oxford, 1957). For intention in relation to language, see H. P. Grice, 'Meaning', *Philosophical Review*, 66 (1957), 377–88, reprinted in P. F. Strawson (ed.), *Oxford Readings in Philosophical Logic*

(Oxford, 1967), pp. 39–48. For the application of some of these ideas to art, see A. J. Close, ' "Don Quixote" and the "Intentionalist" Fallacy', *British Journal of Aesthetics*, 12 (1972), 19–39, reprinted in *On Literary Intention*, pp. 174–93, and A. Savile, 'The Place of Intention in the Concept of Art', *Proceedings of the Aristotelian Society*, 69 (1968–9), 101–24, reprinted in Osborne, pp. 158–76.

8. The connection between formalism and anti-intentionalism is clear in Beardsley's work. See M. C. Beardsley, *Aesthetics: Problems in the Philosophy of Criticism* (2nd edn., Indianapolis, 1981), esp. pp. 17–29. For Beardsley's most recent statement on intention, see 'Intentions and Interpretations: A Fallacy Revived' in his *The Aesthetic Point of View: Selected Essays* (Ithaca and London, 1982), pp. 188–207.

9. As n. 2 above.

10. See G. N. Knauer, 'Vergil's Aeneid and Homer', *Greek, Roman and Byzantine Studies*, 5 (1964), 61–84.

11. ii. 34. 65–6.

12. Cf. MacIntyre, op. cit., ch. 4, esp. pp. 56–60.

13. *Aesthetics: . . . Problems of Criticism*, pp. 25–6.

14. This is a much simplified version of the argument put forward by A. Savile in 'The Place of Intention in the Concept of Art' (Osborne, pp. 167 ff.).

15. For some views which, like mine, stress the fact that works of art are created by particular people at particular times in particular societies but develop this point with greater complexity and sophistication, see K. Walton, 'Categories of Art', *Philosophical Review*, 79 (1970), 334–67, reprinted in Margolis, pp. 88–114; Savile, esp. ch. 4; R. Selden, *Criticism and Objectivity* (London, 1984), chs. 5–7.

16. *Validity in Interpretation* (New Haven and London, 1967). Cf. also *The Aims of Interpretation* (Chicago and London, 1976). Hirsch's view is applied to visual art by E. H. Gombrich, *Symbolic Images: Studies in the Art of the Renaissance* (London, 1972), pp. 1–22.

17. Cf. *Validity in Interpretation*, pp. 227–30. See also Savile, pp. 71–5.

Chapter 8: Meaning and truth

1. *The Stagecraft of Aeschylus* (Oxford, 1977), pp. 1–3; cf. pp. 12 ff. See also N. Coghill, *Shakespeare's Professional Skills* (Cambridge, 1964) ch. 1.

2. *The PreSocratic Philosophers* (2nd edn., London, 1982), p. 465.

3. J. Bayley, *The Characters of Love* (London, 1960), p. 212; A. Calder, introduction to the Penguin English Library edition of

Sir Walter Scott, *Old Mortality* (Harmondsworth, 1975), p. 22. Note that Bayley, like Hirsch, associates meaning with intention.

4. New York edn., ch. 9, p. 217; ch. 22, p. 297.

5. Op. cit., p. 1.

6. *Pagan Mysteries in the Renaissance* (2nd edn., London, 1968), ch. 7, pp. 113–27.

7. *Middlemarch*, bk. 1, ch. 5.

8. In this classification I partly follow Max Black and John Searle, both of whose views on metaphor I discuss. For Max Black's views see 'Metaphor', *Proceedings of the Aristotelian Society*, 55 (1954), 273–94, reprinted in his *Models and Metaphors* (Ithaca, NY, 1962), pp. 25–47 and in M. Johnson (ed.), *Philosophical Perspectives on Metaphor* (Minneapolis, 1981), pp. 63–82, and 'More about Metaphor', *Dialectica*, 31 (1977), 431–57, reprinted in A. Ortony (ed.), *Metaphor and Thought* (Cambridge, 1979), pp. 19–43; cf. also 'How Metaphors Work: A Reply to Donald Davidson', *Critical Inquiry*, 6 (1979), 131–43, reprinted in S. Sacks (ed.), *On Metaphor* (Chicago, 1979), pp. 181–92. For Searle's views see ch. 4 of his *Expression and Meaning* (Cambridge, 1979), also printed in Ortony, pp. 92–123 and in Johnson, pp. 248–85. For the view that there is no such thing as metaphorical meaning, see Donald Davidson, 'What Metaphors Mean', *Critical Inquiry*, 5 (1978), 31–47, reprinted in Sacks, pp. 29–45, in Johnson, pp. 63–82, and in M. Platts (ed.), *Reference, Truth and Reality* (London, 1980), pp. 238–54.

9. Black is influenced by Wittgenstein's account of 'seeing as' here. Cf. Chapter 2 above.

10. See L. J. Cohen in Ortony, op. cit., pp. 65–6.

11. As n. 12 to Chapter 6.

12. See ch. 19 and the 'Finale'. Cf. R. Jenkyns, *The Victorians and Ancient Greece* (Oxford, 1980), p. 127.

13. See O. Cargill, 'Henry James as Freudian Pioneer', *Chicago Review*, 10 (1956), 16.

14. For some further discussion of Marxist interpretation of literature, see Chapter 9.

Chapter 9: Art and morals

1. Cf. Chapter 4 above.

2. Cf. also the conversation between Dorian Gray and Lord Henry Wotton in ch. 19 of the novel and Wilde's essay, 'The Critic as Artist'.

3. See, e.g., Aristophanes, *Frogs*, 830–1533, Plutarch, *How the Young Man Should Study Poetry*, and the discussion in D. A. Russell, *Criticism in Antiquity* (London, 1981), ch. 6.

4. *Republic* III, 386a–392b.

5. Ibid. X, 602c–606d; *Ion*, 535c–e.

6. Cf. Chapter 2, where *Republic* X is discussed. I am here ignoring the differences between Plato's view of imitation in *Republic* X and his view in *Republic* II and III. On these see, in the first instance, R. C. Cross and A. D. Woozley, *Plato's Republic: A Philosophical Commentary* (London, 1964), ch. 12.

7. See B. Williams (ed.), *Obscenity and Film Censorship: An Abridgement of the Williams Report* (Cambridge, 1981), ch. 6 and ch. 9, p. 20 ff. The argument in the report concerns the effects of classes·of material, not of individual books or films, since only classes of material can be banned by the law (ch. 5, p. 34). However, most of the points made apply with equal force to the effects of individual works.

8. See, e.g., G. Steiner, 'To Civilize our Gentlemen', *Language and Silence* (London, 1967), pp. 75–88; T. Eagleton, *Criticism and Ideology* (London, 1976), p. 16.

9. For more comprehensive accounts see D. Forgacs, 'Marxist Literary Theories' in A. Jefferson and D. Robey (eds.), *Modern Literary Theory* (2nd edn. London, 1986), pp. 166–203; D. Laing, *The Marxist Theory of Art* (Hassocks, Sussex, 1978); T. Eagleton, *Marxism and Literary Criticism* (London, 1976).

10. Marx himself made the distinction between base and superstructure in the preface to *A Contribution to the Critique of Political Economy* (first published, 1859).

11. See G. Lukács, *The Meaning of Contemporary Realism* (London, 1963). Cf. Chapter 6 above.

12. See J. Willett (ed.), *Brecht on Theatre* (New York, 1964) and B. Brecht, 'Against Georg Lukács', *New Left Review*, 84 (1974), 39–53 (four short essays originally written in 1938).

13. P. Macherey, *A Theory of Literary Production* (London, 1978), a translation of *Pour une théorie de la production littéraire* (Paris, 1966). For the relationship of Macherey's view to structuralism, see D. Forgacs, loc. cit., pp. 177–83.

14. See esp. *Criticism and Ideology*.

15. *The Rape of Clarissa* (Oxford, 1982), pp. 24–5.

16. Eagleton, *Criticism and Ideology*, pp. 118–21. This and some other Marxist interpretations of George Eliot are discussed by C. Butler, *Interpretation, Deconstruction and Ideology* (Oxford, 1984), pp. 110–36.

17. R. H. Super (ed.), *English Literature and Irish Politics* (Ann Arbor, 1973), p. 161.

18. Ibid., p. 171. Cf. also the essay on Wordsworth in the same volume of the Super edition, pp. 36–55.

19.　*The Great Tradition* (2nd edn., London, 1960), p. 8.

20.　*Revaluation* (London, 1936), chs. 5–7.

21.　pp. 159–60 and 168.

22.　p. 257.

23.　p. 123.

24.　For further discussion of the positions of Arnold and Leavis, see V. Buckley, *Poetry and Morality* (London, 1959) and J. Casey, *The Language of Criticism* (London, 1966), chs. 8 and 9.

25.　Cf. R. W. Beardsmore, *Art and Morality* (London, 1971), pp. 53–75; Savile, ch. 5.

26.　C. Day Lewis (ed.), *The Collected Poems of Wilfred Owen* (London, 1963), p. 12.

Further Reading

Classics

Plato, *Republic* II, III and X; *Ion.* There are many translations of the *Republic.* I recommend the Penguin by H. D. P. Lee (1955) or the World's Classics translation by Robin Waterfield (1993). There are translations of the *Ion* by D. A. Russell in D. A. Russell and M. Winterbottom (eds.), *Classical Literary Criticism* (The World's Classics, Oxford, 1989) and by P. Woodruff in *Two Comic Dialogues: Ion and Hippias Major* (Library of Liberal Arts, Indianapolis, 1983).

Aristotle, *Poetics.* There are many translations. I recommend the Penguin by T. S. Dorsch in *Classical Literary Criticism: Aristotle, Horace, Longinus* (1965) or the translation by M. E. Hubbard in the World's Classics *Classical Literary Criticism.*

I. Kant, *Critique of Aesthetic Judgement* (first published, 1790). The standard English translations are by J. H. Bernard (2nd edn., London, 1914) and J. C. Meredith (Oxford, 1952). The first part only, 'The Analytic of the Beautiful', has also been translated by W. Cerf (Library of Liberal Arts, Indianapolis, 1963). For some discussion of Kant's aesthetics, see S. Körner, *Kant* (Harmondsworth, 1955), ch. 8; D. W. Crawford, *Kant's Aesthetic Theory* (Madison, Wisconsin, 1974); M. Warnock, *Imagination* (London and Boston, 1976), Part II.

A. Schopenhauer, *The World as Will and Representation,* trans. E. J. F. Payne (Indian Hills, Colorado, 1958). There is also an older translation by R. B. Haldane and J. Kemp under the title, *The World as Will and Idea* (London, 1883). For a discussion of Schopenhauer's aesthetics, see P. Gardiner, *Schopenhauer* (Harmondsworth, 1963), ch. 5.

G. W. F. Hegel, *Aesthetics: lectures on fine art,* trans. T. M. Knox (Oxford, 1975); Hegel's aesthetics are expounded and discussed by S. Bungay, *Beauty and Truth* (Oxford, 1984).

E. Hanslick, *The Beautiful in Music* (first published in German, 1854). The English translation by G. Cohen (1891) is most readily available in the Library of Liberal Arts series (New York, 1957). This edition has been used for all quotations and references in the text. Extracts from Hanslick's criticism may be found in S. Deas, *In Defence of Hanslick* (2nd edn., Farnborough, 1972), chs. 5–7; a selection from his critical writings has been published as *Vienna's Golden Years of Music. 1850–1900*, translated and edited by H. Pleasants (New York, 1950; London, 1951).

L. Tolstoy, *What is Art?*, trans. A. Maude (London, 1898).

B. Croce, *Aesthetic*, trans. D. Ainslie (2nd edn., London, 1922); *Breviary of Aesthetics*, translated as *The Essence of Aesthetic*, by D. Ainslie (London, 1921), also available as *Guide to Aesthetics*, trans. P. Romanell (South Bend, Ind., 1979, reprinted Lanham, Md., 1983); article on Aesthetics in the 14th edn. of the *Encyclopaedia Britannica* (1928), reprinted under the title 'Aesthetica in Nuce' in *Philosophy, Poetry, History: An anthology of essays by B. Croce*, trans. C. Sprigge (London, 1966).

C. Bell, *Art* (London, 1914). For examples of his criticism, see *Since Cézanne* (London, 1922) and *Landmarks in Nineteenth-Century Painting* (London, 1927).

R. Fry, *Vision and Design* (London, 1920); *Transformations* (London, 1926); *Last Lectures* (Cambridge, 1939).

R. G. Collingwood, *The Principles of Art* (Oxford, 1938).

Modern works

M. C. Beardsley, *Aesthetics: Problems in the Philosophy of Criticism* (2nd edn., Indianapolis, 1981).

M. Budd, *Music and the Emotions* (London, 1985).

E. H. Gombrich, *Art and Illusion* (London, 1960). Many of the themes of this book are more briefly discussed in the title essay of Gombrich, *Meditations on a Hobby Horse* (London, 1963).

S. Langer, *Feeling and Form* (London, 1953).

A. Savile, *The Test of Time* (Oxford, 1982).

R. Scruton, *Art and Imagination* (London, 1974); *The Aesthetics of Architecture* (London, 1979).

R. Wollheim, *Art and Its Objects* (2nd edn., Cambridge, 1980).

Much work in aesthetics, as in other areas of philosophy, is published in the form of articles in specialist journals. Useful collections of articles include:

H. Osborne (ed.), *Aesthetics* (Oxford Readings in Philosophy, Oxford, 1972).

J. Margolis (ed.), *Philosophy Looks at the Arts* (revised edn., Temple University, Pa., 1978).

The second half of this book touches on questions discussed in literary theory. An expansion in this field in recent years has been followed by the publication of a number of introductions. Among these I recommend:

A. Jefferson and D. Robey (eds.), *Modern Literary Theory: A Comparative Introduction* (2nd edn., London, 1986).

R. Selden, *A Reader's Guide to Contemporary Literary Theory* (Brighton, 1985).

Index

OPUS

General Editors

Walter Bodmer   Christopher Butler   Robert Evans

OPUS books provide concise, original, and authoritative introductions to a wide range of subjects in the humanities and sciences. They are written by experts for the general reader as well as for students.

Economics and Business Studies

The State and the Economic System
An Introduction to the History of Political Economy
Phyllis Deane

The Way People Work
Job Satisfaction and the Challenge of Change
Christine Howarth

Democracy at Work
Tom Schuller

History

The Industrial Revolution 1760–1830 2/e
T. S. Ashton

Rebellion or Revolution?
England 1640–1660
G. E. Aylmer

Early Modern France 1560–1715
Robin Briggs

Modern Spain
Raymond Carr

The Workshop of the World
British Economic History 1820–1880 2/e
J. D. Chambers

The Economy of England 1450–1750
Donald C. Coleman

The Impact of English Towns 1700–1800
P. J. Corfield

The Russian Revolution
Sheila Fitzpatrick

War in European History
Michael Howard

The Medieval Expansion of Europe
J. R. S. Phillips

The First World War
Keith Robbins

The French Revolution
J. M. Roberts

The Voice of the Past
Oral History 2/e
Paul Thompson

Town, City, and Nation
England 1850–1914
P. J. Waller

Law

Law and Modern Society
P. S. Atiyah

Introduction to English Law 9/e
William Geldart

The Lawful Rights of Mankind
An Introduction to the International
   Legal Code of Human Rights
Paul Sieghart

Literature

The Modern American Novel
Malcolm Bradbury

The English Language
R. W. Burchfield

Ancient Greek Literature
K. J. Dover

Shakespeare
A Writer's Progress
Philip Edwards

Linguistic Criticism
Roger Fowler

British Theatre since 1955
A Reassessment
Ronald Hayman

Modern English Literature
W. W. Robson

Structuralism and Since
From Lévi-Strauss to Derrida
John Sturrock

English Literature and its Background

This Stageplay World
English Literature and its Background
   1580–1625
Julia Briggs

Medieval Writers and their Work
Middle English Literature and its
   Background 1100–1500
J. A. Burrow

Romantics, Rebels and Reactionaries
English Literature and its Background
1760–1830
Marilyn Butler

Philosophy

Aristotle the Philosopher
J. L. Ackrill

Metaphysics
The Logical Approach
José A. Benardete

Karl Marx
His Life and Environment 4/e
Isaiah Berlin

The Standing of Psychoanalysis
B. A. Farrell

The Character of Mind
Colin McGinn

Understanding Plato
David J. Melling

Moral Philosophy
D. D. Raphael

The Problems of Philosophy
Bertrand Russell

Aesthetics
An Introduction to the Philosophy of
    Art
Anne Sheppard

Ethics since 1900 3/e
Mary Warnock

Existentialism
Mary Warnock

Philosophy and the Brain
J. Z. Young

A History of Western Philosophy

The Rationalists: Volume 4
John Cottingham

Classical Thought: Volume 1
Terence Irwin

Continental Philosophy since 1750:
    Volume 7
The Rise and Fall of the Self
Robert C. Solomon

The Empiricists: Volume 5
R. S. Woolhouse

Politics and International Affairs

Devolution
Vernon Bogdanor

Marx's Social Theory
Terrell Carver

Philosophers and Pamphleteers
Political Theorists of the
    Enlightenment
Maurice Cranston

International Relations in a Changing
    World 4/e
Joseph Frankel

Contemporary International Theory and
    the Behaviour of States
Joseph Frankel

The Life and Times of Liberal
    Democracy
C. B. Macpherson

Socialisms
Theories and Practices
Anthony Wright

Religion

Christianity in the West 1400–1700
John Bossy

Judaism
Nicholas de Lange

An Introduction to the Philosophy of Religion
Brian Davies

Islam
A Historical Survey 2/e
H. A. R. Gibb

Modern Theology
A Sense of Direction
James P. Mackey

Religion and the People of Western Europe
Hugh McLeod

Roman Catholicism in England from the Elizabethan Settlement to the Second Vatican Council
Edward Norman

What is Theology?
Maurice Wiles

Hinduism 2/e
R. C. Zaehner

Science

What is Psychotherapy?
Sidney Bloch

The Philosophies of Science
An Introductory Survey 2/e
Rom Harré

A Historical Introduction to the Philosophy of Science 2/e
John Losee

The Making of the Atomic Age
Alwyn McKay

The Primeval Universe
Jayant V. Narlikar

The Structure of the Universe
Jayant V. Narlikar

What is Ecology? 2/e
Denis F. Owen

Energy
A Guide Book
Janet Ramage

The Problems of Science

The Problems of Physics
A. J. Leggett

The Problems of Biology
John Maynard Smith

The Problems of Chemistry
W. G. Richards

The Problems of Evolution
Mark Ridley

The Problems of Mathematics
Ian Stewart

Social Sciences

Thinking about Peace and War
Martin Ceadel

*Science and Technology in World
    Development*
Robin Clarke

Changes in British Society 3/e
A. H. Halsey

*Urban Planning in Rich and Poor
    Countries*
Hugh Stretton

Crime and Criminology
A Critical Introduction
Nigel Walker

Policing Liberal Society
Steve Uglow

OXFORD

MORE OXFORD PAPERBACKS

This book is just one of nearly 1000 Oxford Paperbacks currently in print. If you would like details of other Oxford Paperbacks, including titles in the World's Classics, Oxford Reference, Oxford Books, OPUS, Past Masters, Oxford Authors, and Oxford Shakespeare series, please write to:

UK and Europe: Oxford Paperbacks Publicity Manager, Arts and Reference Publicity Department, Oxford University Press, Walton Street, Oxford OX2 6DP.

Customers in UK and Europe will find Oxford Paperbacks available in all good bookshops. But in case of difficulty please send orders to the Cash-with-Order Department, Oxford University Press Distribution Services, Saxon Way West, Corby, Northants NN18 9ES. Tel: 0536 741519; Fax: 0536 746337. Please send a cheque for the total cost of the books, plus £1.75 postage and packing for orders under £20; £2.75 for orders over £20. Customers outside the UK should add 10% of the cost of the books for postage and packing.

USA: Oxford Paperbacks Marketing Manager, Oxford University Press, Inc., 200 Madison Avenue, New York, N.Y. 10016.

Canada: Trade Department, Oxford University Press, 70 Wynford Drive, Don Mills, Ontario M3C 1J9.

Australia: Trade Marketing Manager, Oxford University Press, G.P.O. Box 2784Y, Melbourne 3001, Victoria.

South Africa: Oxford University Press, P.O. Box 1141, Cape Town 8000.

OPUS

General Editors: Walter Bodmer,
Christopher Butler, Robert Evans,
John Skorupski

CLASSICAL THOUGHT

Terence Irwin

Spanning over a thousand years from Homer to Saint Augustine, *Classical Thought* encompasses a vast range of material, in succinct style, while remaining clear and lucid even to those with no philosophical or Classical background.

The major philosophers and philosophical schools are examined—the Presocratics, Socrates, Plato, Aristotle, Stoicism, Epicureanism, Neoplatonism; but other important thinkers, such as Greek tragedians, historians, medical writers, and early Christian writers, are also discussed. The emphasis is naturally on questions of philosophical interest (although the literary and historical background to Classical philosophy is not ignored), and again the scope is broad—ethics, the theory of knowledge, philosophy of mind, philosophical theology. All this is presented in a fully integrated, highly readable text which covers many of the most important areas of ancient thought and in which stress is laid on the variety and continuity of philosophical thinking after Aristotle.

OPUS

General Editors: Walter Bodmer
Christopher Butler, Robert Evans,
John Skorupski

METROPOLIS

Emrys Jones

Past civilizations have always expressed themselves in great cities, immense in size, wealth, and in their contribution to human progress. We are still enthralled by ancient cities like Babylon, Rome, and Constantinople. Today, giant cities abound, but some are pre-eminent. As always, they represent the greatest achievements of different cultures. But increasingly, they have also been drawn into a world economic system as communications have improved.

Metropolis explores the idea of a class of supercities in the past and in the present, and in the western and developing worlds. It analyses the characteristics they share as well as those that make them unique; the effect of technology on their form and function; and the problems that come with size—congestion, poverty and inequality, squalor—that are sobering contrasts to the inherent glamour and attraction of great cities throughout time.

PHILOSOPHY IN OXFORD PAPERBACKS
THE GREAT PHILOSOPHERS

Bryan Magee

Beginning with the death of Socrates in 399, and following the story through the centuries to recent figures such as Bertrand Russell and Wittgenstein, Bryan Magee and fifteen contemporary writers and philosophers provide an accessible and exciting introduction to Western philosophy and its greatest thinkers.

Bryan Magee in conversation with:

A. J. Ayer	John Passmore
Michael Ayers	Anthony Quinton
Miles Burnyeat	John Searle
Frederick Copleston	Peter Singer
Hubert Dreyfus	J. P. Stern
Anthony Kenny	Geoffrey Warnock
Sidney Morgenbesser	Bernard Williams
Martha Nussbaum	

'Magee is to be congratulated . . . anyone who sees the programmes or reads the book will be left in no danger of believing philosophical thinking is unpractical and uninteresting.' Ronald Hayman, *Times Educational Supplement*

'one of the liveliest, fast-paced introductions to philosophy, ancient and modern that one could wish for' *Universe*

ILLUSTRATED HISTORIES IN OXFORD PAPERBACKS

THE OXFORD ILLUSTRATED HISTORY OF ENGLISH LITERATURE

Edited by Pat Rogers

Britain possesses a literary heritage which is almost unrivalled in the Western world. In this volume, the richness, diversity, and continuity of that tradition are explored by a group of Britain's foremost literary scholars.

Chapter by chapter the authors trace the history of English literature, from its first stirrings in Anglo-Saxon poetry to the present day. At its heart towers the figure of Shakespeare, who is accorded a special chapter to himself. Other major figures such as Chaucer, Milton, Donne, Wordsworth, Dickens, Eliot, and Auden are treated in depth, and the story is brought up to date with discussion of living authors such as Seamus Heaney and Edward Bond.

'[a] lovely volume . . . put in your thumb and pull out plums' Michael Foot

'scholarly and enthusiastic people have written inspiring essays that induce an eagerness in their readers to return to the writers they admire' *Economist*

OXFORD REFERENCE

THE CONCISE OXFORD COMPANION TO ENGLISH LITERATURE

Edited by Margaret Drabble and Jenny Stringer

Based on the immensely popular fifth edition of the *Oxford Companion to English Literature* this is an indispensable, compact guide to the central matter of English literature.

There are more than 5,000 entries on the lives and works of authors, poets, playwrights, essayists, philosophers, and historians; plot summaries of novels and plays; literary movements; fictional characters; legends; theatres; periodicals; and much more.

The book's sharpened focus on the English literature of the British Isles makes it especially convenient to use, but there is still generous coverage of the literature of other countries and of other disciplines which have influenced or been influenced by English literature.

From reviews of *The Oxford Companion to English Literature*:

'a book which one turns to with constant pleasure . . . a book with much style and little prejudice' Iain Gilchrist, *TLS*

'it is quite difficult to imagine, in this genre, a more useful publication' Frank Kermode, *London Review of Books*

'incarnates a living sense of tradition . . . sensitive not to fashion merely but to the spirit of the age' Christopher Ricks, *Sunday Times*